HOME TANNING AND LEATHER MAKING GUIDE

A BOOK OF INFORMATION FOR THOSE WHO
WISH TO TAN AND MAKE LEATHER FROM
CATTLE, HORSE, CALF, SHEEP, GOAT,
DEER AND OTHER HIDES A N D
SKINS; ALSO EXPLAINS HOW
TO SKIN, HANDLE, CLAS-
SIFY AND MARKET

By

ALBERT B. FARNHAM

Tanner and Taxidermist

PUBLISHED BY
A. R. HARDING
COLUMBUS, OHIO

A. R. Harding Publishing Co.

2878 East Main Street

Columbus, Ohio 43209

ISBN   0-936622-11-3

ALBERT B. FARNHAM, *Author*

CONTENTS

LIST OF ILLUSTRATIONS

INTRODUCTORY

EATHER in some form has been in use from mankind's earliest days to the present, and although there are many ingenious and valuable imitations and substitutes, the saying "There's nothing like leather" is as true as ever. Generally the present day tannery is a factory provided with expensive machines, operated by skilled help under direction of some one with considerable knowledge of chemistry.

Still the fact remains that good useful leather can be profitably made by hand under some conditions. The isolated rancher or farmer who cannot himself convert some of his hides into leather, is in the position of a woodsman depending on a distant woodworking mill for building material, rather than hew timbers, saw planks and split clapboards and shingles with his own hands.

The United States Department of Agriculture, which has received in the last two years thousands of requests for directions for making leather, say in regard to this situation:

"Normally the tanning of a few hides or skins by the inexperienced and without adequate facilities cannot be recommended either from the viewpoint of national economy or of individual profit. The tanners know how and are equipped to make all the leather the country needs. They can make better leather more economically than the farmer can. There comes a time, however, as has been the case during the past year or more, when the products of the farm and the ranch sell for less than the cost of production; when 'country' hides for example could hardly be given away, yet when leather in small pieces cost the farmer 50 cents to $1.50 a pound. Under these conditions the farmer and the rancher naturally feel that they must attempt to work up their farm raw materials or otherwise do without the finished products therefrom."

The Bureau of Chemistry, under their direction, have furnished directions for tanning a hide or two as sole or harness leather with such equipment as is within reach on the farm and ranch.

Other tried processes have been added to these and the whole is presented as an aid to the class which is said to be helped by Heaven, those who help themselves.

The directions and the amount of material here given are for preparing one large or medium skin of from forty to seventy pounds weight of cow or steer, or three small skins like heavy calf. For smaller skins make one-half or one-fourth the quantity in the same proportion.

No doubt at first you will often fail to attain satisfactory results, but each attempt should add to experience and reduce the chance of subsequent failures. Small scale operations will not produce leather equal in appearance and perhaps in quality to most of that on the market, but it should be possible to make leather which will be of much service for a great many purposes. These directions may be modified as needed to suit conditions, particularly as to the equipment at hand.

Complete success will depend largely on the ingenuity and perseverance of the worker. There is a rather popular idea current that the secret of tanning is some chemical or grease which makes the stiff hides soft as a glove. Elbow grease is what has most to do with leather making.

Albert B. Farnham.

CHAPTER I

SELECTION OF HIDES AND SKINS

HE kind of leather which can be made from a hide or skin depends chiefly on its size or weight, especially when worked up by hand methods. Splitting machines can convert a heavy hide into two or more layers of light leather, which is impossible to the hand workman. The most he can do is to reduce a skin to uniform thickness by shaving down the thicker parts.

Hides, as the skins of the larger and adult animals are called, are suited for sole, harness, belting or heavy leathers. Smaller animals such as sheep, calves, goats, deer, etc., furnish what are classed as skins, making light and fancy leathers such as are used in shoes, gloves, bags or garments. The usual domesticated farm and range animals are the most important sources of supply for hides and skins, with the exception of such as are used as furs.

In selecting skins for different kinds of leather it may be taken as a general rule that the thickness of the finished leather will be a little more than that of the untanned hide. Raw hides and skins of domestic animals are classified by buyers and tanners about as follows:

Heavy steers and cows,	60 lbs. and over.
Medium steers and cows,	40 to 60 lbs.
Kip or yearling,	15 to 25 lbs.
Calf,	8 to 15 lbs.
Light calf,	7 to 8 lbs.
Deacon calf,	7 lbs. or less.
Shrunk calf,	Very light.
Bull hides (all weights),	Separate class.
Horse Hides,	Large.
Pony and Colt Hides,	Small.
Hog,	As to size & quality.

They are further classified in regard to their curing as green, green salted, dry salted, and flint dry. A green hide is as taken off the animal, without salting or curing of any kind; green salted is a hide which has been salted folded or spread out from twenty-four hours to six months, but not dried out; while a dry salt is one so salted but spread and dried out as it will do in ten days to two weeks. A flint hide is dried out without salting. The weights given refer to green hides; a flint dry is about one-half the weight of the same green; a dry salted about two-thirds; and a green salted about five-sixths. For example, a green hide weighing 60 lbs. drops to 50 lbs. green salted, 40 lbs. dry salted, and 30 lbs. flint dry.

Sheep skins known as pelts are classified chiefly by the weight of wool they bear. Those lately sheared have a low value. The pelts from sheep dead of disease are of value chiefly for the wool, as the leather from them is very inferior.

Goat skins properly prepared furnish a good light leather, and those of the Angora variety are often tanned with the fleece on for use as rugs. Some of the finest are even made up as ladies' furs. Few skins of the common goat are tanned with the hair on, most of the goat skin robes and rugs used in this country being imported from North China.

Deer skins are chiefly tanned as buckskin for glove leather. (Also many, many sheep furnish so called buckskin, too.) Very infrequently the skin of an alligator, snake or fish is tanned, mostly for ornament, though alligator is one of the most durable of leathers.

To make sole, harness or heavy belt leather

requires hides of 50 lbs. weight or over. Lace leather needs hides of from 20 to 40 lbs., depending on the thickness desired. Such skins of yearlings and light cows are also suitable for small belting and straps. Thin or light calf make good boot and shoe uppers or heavy glove stock.

The thickest parts of a hide are the neck and a strip down the back. Heavy hides are usually, for easy handling, cut down the back and each side split again into two "strips." The back "strip" makes the heaviest leather and is about twice as wide as the belly strip, if split where it should be, at the break of the flank. Thus a hide furnishes two sides or four strips of leather of varying thickness. This way if desirable the heavy part of a hide can be tanned as sole, and the lighter strips, of course, as lace or harness leather.

It goes without saying that if you wish to make the best leather you must have good hides to start with, still an inferior or damaged hide will afford practice for the beginner, and when more proficient he can take over better material. You can make just as *good* leather from hides

LEATHER FROM AN IMPROPERLY CURED HIDE

Such a hide is scarcely worth tanning, as it will make only inferior soles and lifts; properly cured it would have given 6 to 8 pairs of good outsoles.

damaged by cuts, scores or grub holes, but the
piece of leather will be worth much less on account of these damaged places.

The best hides for leather purposes are those
of summer and fall take off.   There are several
good reasons for this.   It depletes the hide sub-
stance to grow the heavier winter coat of hair,
winter hides are less firm and heavier hair retaining more moisture to retard curing.   Salt
also acts more quickly in warm weather.   Summer deer skins, though making the best buckskin, are fortunately not to be had nowadays
on account of the protection of the game laws.

The same reason which detracts from the
value of a hide for leather, makes it preferable
for use as a robe or rug.   Such skins are preferred on account of their light weight com-
pared with their spread, as a heavy hide would
require too much thinning down.

Goat and sheep to be tanned with hair or wool
on should be carefully selected.   Those with
matted or tangled fleece or filled with burrs and
chaff should be made into leather, as such fleeces
seldom can be put in good order.

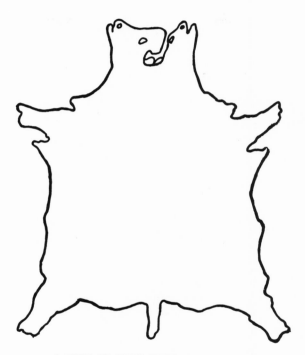

A HIDE OF GOOD PATTERN AND TRIM

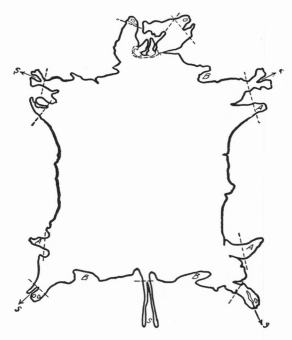

A HIDE OF POOR PATTERN AND TRIM

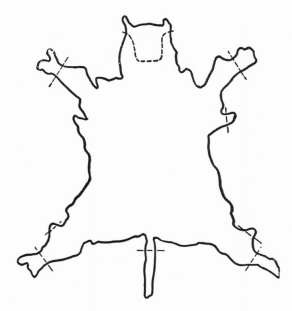

A CALFSKIN OF GOOD PATTERN AND TRIM
The dotted lines indicate amount cut off before tanning.

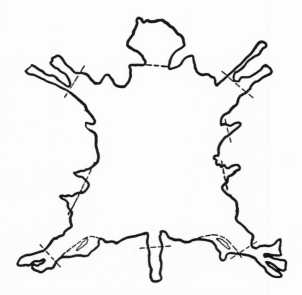

A CALFSKIN OF POOR PATTERN AND TRIM

The dotted lines show the excessive amount of trimming necessary because of the poor pattern. The head and practically all of each shank must be cut off.

CHAPTER II

F YOU wish to make good leather you must have good hides to start with, and the first step towards good leather is the proper removal of the hide from the carcass.   In the case of cattle proceed as follows:

1. Cut from the base of left horn past the left eye to the nose, then across between the horns and skin the face.

2. Cut from the under lip down the throat and along the center of belly to the base of tail.

3. Split up the inside of all four legs to the body and sever skin at the feet (hoofs).

4. Skin on both sides of body to the tail, split and skin the tail and starting the hide at base of tail, remove by pulling and use of the knife, using care not to cut or score.

5. After taking off, spread the hide out long enough for the animal heat to escape.

Allow six or eight hours or over night to cool. Do not do this on the ground. Use a wooden or cement floor or a few poles nailed to trestles or something similar.

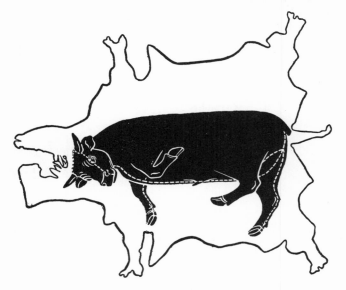

PROPER RIPPING OPEN CUTS FOR A CORRECT PATTERN

The dotted lines show the path of the knife, and the solid lines show the appearance of the hide when spread out.

As soon as cooled, such skin can be started in process of tanning, or by curing they can be held several months. This is sometimes desirable in order to make selection or accumulate more skins before beginning. Also, when they are to be held for sale as raw hides they should be given some sort of curing.

SALTING HIDES: When cooled and spread out flesh side up on a level place, cover the flesh side evenly with salt. To salt well requires at least one-half the weight of hide in salt. That is, an 80 lb. hide needs about 40 lbs. of salt altogether; more will not hurt. Use coarse salt for hides and fine salt for skins, (calf, etc.).

Leave the hide with flesh side covered with salt, undisturbed for at least two days. Then if you wish to ship it at once it may be turned over and rubbed with salt on hair side, folded and rolled up flesh side out and packed in a box. This is green salted very heavy and will drip considerable moisture. It requires about thirty days to produce a salt cured hide, which will be about 15% lighter than the green hide. If after the hide has been spread out salted two or three days the water be drained off, it may be left spread on floor or hung over poles until quite dry, which will be in two to four weeks. In this condition hides may be packed away in a cool cellar or some such place, through the fall, winter and spring months without any other preparation.

This gives opportunity to select skins for tanning and to sell whenever prices are favorable. Such hides can not be safely kept after May or June unless poisoned with an arsenical solution. This solution is made as follows:

Powdered Arsenic ....10 lbs.
Concentrated Lye.........................4 oz.
Water..8 gals.

or smaller quantities in proportion. Mix the arsenic and lye with the water in a tub or jar and let it stand several days, five or six, say. Mix one part of this solution with five parts water and apply to both sides of the hides with a brush or better, a sprayer. I hardly need add the caution that this solution be kept away from stock or children, as it is, of course, very poisonous. Unless treated in some such manner, hides will be riddled with holes or entirely eaten up by the dermestes or bacon beetle during the summer months.

Any cut 6 inches from edge of hide reduces it in value one grade, as will also five scores or one score where the nail can be pushed through. Places rubbed by dragging reduce one grade. Brands and grub holes are also reckoned as damages, as they mar the leather for many uses,

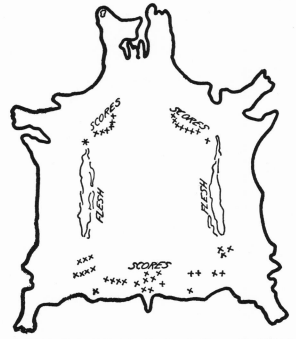

A POORLY TAKEN OFF HIDE, SCORED AND FLESH
LEFT ON

Scores (cuts) are very numerous around the tail and hind
quarters, which is the most valuable section of the hide.
Careful knife work will prevent these defects.

as do the spots where ticks have bitten the cattle.

Sheep skins require careful handling. They should be carefully salted with clean, fine salt, two quarts to the pelt in summer. Turn them frequently to avoid heating and do not put in large piles. Horse hides decay quickly and should be skinned promptly and thoroughly salted when cool. Avoid damaging the grain by dragging or rubbing the hair side when moving dead animals.

DONT'S FOR HIDE HANDLERS

Don't cut your hides in skinning them. Every cut in the hide lessens the value and *you* are the loser.

Don't leave a lot of meat sticking to a hide.

Don't let hides lay in a pile after skinning. One hour or so may damage them. Spread out at once.

Don't be stingy with salt. Another five cents worth may save a couple of dollars in the end. Salt all parts well; look out for wrinkles and folds stuck together.

Don't think because you have sprinkled salt

on a hide it is salt cured.   It takes several days and lots of salt to do it.

While, as we have said, the hide may go to process once it is cooled, many tanners wish to have all hides salted, as they claim the salt helps open the skin and draws out unnecessary moisture.   Deer skins should not be salted.   If you wish to keep them a while before tanning, stretch them to full extent in a pole frame and dry in the air and shade.

Never try to dry any skins by pegging out on the ground.   There is always some moisture in the earth, and they cannot be hung up out of reach of dogs and other animals if pegged out. Make a rectangular frame of sufficient size by nailing or tying four poles together at the corners and fasten the skin in this with a bagging needle and twine.   A thong can be used by passing it through small slits close to edges of skin. Use four pieces of twine or thongs and after lacing, tighten first one and then another opposite until stretched tight.   Do not stretch the head and legs out long, but stretch them into the body by doing it first.   This is a good way to cure skins of deer, calf and pig as well as some of the larger fur animals like bear, wolves, puma, etc.

Sheep and goat skins are thin and the knife must be used carefully on them to avoid cuts. Sheep skins heat so easily, extra care must be taken to thoroughly cool before salting them and after salting to dry them out completely before attempting to store them away.

When removing hides have good sharp knives, common butcher knives will do, though at least one of the regular skinning pattern with curved blade will be useful. After beginning the skinning of large and medium sized animals, especially if they are to be used as food, it is well to hang the carcass up in some way. This not only keeps the meat hide clean, but makes it much easier for the operator, as he can work in an upright position. The animal is usually hung by the hind legs, a gambrel stick being thrust under the tendons at the hocks and a piece of rope or chain used to suspend it. Lacking a block and falls, a tripod will enable one man to hang up most animals. Make this of three stout poles several feet longer than the animal you are skinning, and after lashing or chaining together at one end, arrange them over the carcass with the lower ends widely separated and the gambrel chain made fast to the tops.

Thus by lifting and carrying in the bottom of each pole in turn the base of the tripod is reduced in size and its height increased until the animal is lifted free of the ground.

Small animals like sheep or calves may be hung up on hooks or a tree limb with less trouble.

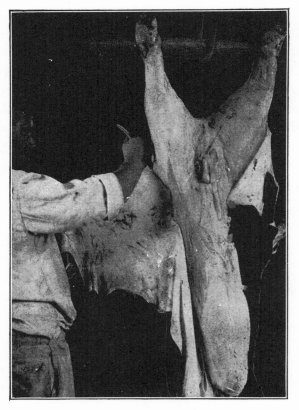

"POUNDING OFF" A CALFSKIN, USING THE BUTT
OF THE KNIFE HANDLE

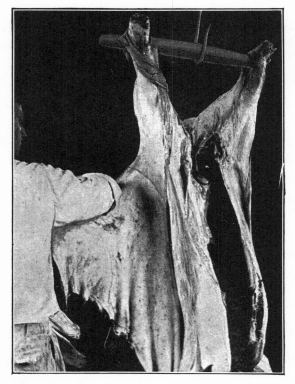

"PULLING OFF" A CALFSKIN

Stretch the skin with the left hand and press down on it with
the right forearm.

CHAPTER III

ANNING is usually best done in some place having a fairly uniform temperature. During storage or tanning hides should not be subject to heating or freezing. If done during spring or fall almost any shed or outbuilding will answer; during winter or summer a cellar or barn basement which will be fairly warm in winter and cool in summer is best. For economy of labor the water supply should be near by and also a drain where the spent tan liquor and water used in washing and rinsing can be disposed of. Use care in emptying the tanning solutions, as while they are not poisonous to the touch, if drunk by live stock some of them would prove fatal and all of them are rather harmful to the soil. On the other hand, the water from liming is beneficial, especially to acid soils.

Dealers in tanners' supplies sell tools in great variety, but for the tanning of a few hides it is possible to use tools that are extemporized or already on hand. Some of these can be made by the general blacksmith and others by yourself. It is possible but not always profitable to make leather with very primitive tools.

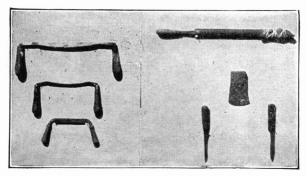

DRAW KNIVES AND OTHER TOOLS
Set of three draw knives—some sharp, others blunt on edge (left). Right, home made tools—rasp, one end wound for grip; small ax, head used as stake or slicker; butcher knives.

In early days the "tan trough" was a part of the equipment on many farms, being merely a section of tree trunk, hollowed out with fire and tools. In this day, however, barrels and tubs are easily procured for such use. All of the operations of soaking, liming, washing and tanning can be carried on in good tight wooden barrels of the usual 40 to 50 gallon size, of which it is well to have at least two, though one

can be made to do in a pinch.   Some half barrels, tubs and wooden buckets are handy also.
One large or medium hide or two or three small
skins is all that can be tanned at the same time
in one barrel.   Half barrels or tubs answer very
nicely for small skins.   Lard or butter tubs and
candy pails may be purchased cheaply when
empty at grocery stores.   It is well to give them
and the barrels also a good coat of paint on the
outside at least, to prevent the hoops rusting, as
rust will stain and discolor the leather as well
as destroy the iron hoops.

   A beam is one requisite of every tanner.   The
Indian or backwoodsman used a fallen tree,
probably, and a good one can be made of a big
hardwood slab, or failing that, a plank.   It
should be seven or eight feet long, ten inches
wide and rounded and smooth on the upper side.
The usual way is to bore two holes about two
feet from one end and fit in them legs of such
a length as to bring that end against the operator's chest or waist.   The other end rests on
the floor.   Another plan is to fasten the beam
horizontally on two posts set firmly in the
ground and cut off at the proper height.   This

makes a very fine beam to work on, but cannot be moved about and set to one side out of the way as the trestle style can. Use care in getting

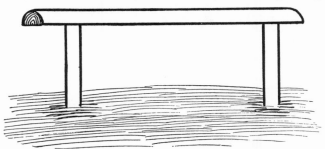

HIDE BEAM, NOT ADJUSTABLE. GOOD FOR LARGE HIDES

a smooth surface on the beam; bumps or ridges in it will cause cuts and holes when skins are beamed.

A good solid table with a plank top and fastened down securely should be part of the working outfit if possible, as it is nearly as important as the beam.

Several long wooden paddles should be on hand to use in stirring solutions, as such stirring is necessary at intervals. In fact, commercial tanners greatly shorten tanning processes by their "paddle vats," which are constantly stirred and agitated by means of power.

For hanging hides in the various liquids, prepare several smooth sticks, pieces of old broom

handles are good, of a length to be an easy fit crosswise of the barrels used and with a loop of heavy cord or small rope fastened to each end of them. When the hides are suspended on these at the right height, the loops can be hooked over nails driven in the outside of the barrel. With these sticks it is easy to adjust, remove or plunge the hides or strips and at the same time keep them flat and free from folds.

STICKS, STRINGS AND BARREL

Showing arrangement for hanging hides in place in barrel.

A cheap scrub brush is handy to use in cleaning skins, and a couple of flat paint brushes for applying color and oil dressing are necessary.

The fleshing knife is also a prime necessity when any skins or hides are dressed. The dealers in tanner's tools sell several patterns of such knives, but one can be contrived that will do, though it will not equal the regular tool. A drawing knife with about a twelve inch blade does very well, if the edge is a little blunted, or an old rasp or file can be drawn out and ground to a blunt edge. The upper end of the rasp should be worked into a tang to hold a second handle at right angles to the regular one. This prevents the knife turning in the hand while in use. A section of old scythe blade can be worked up in the same way and such a knife can

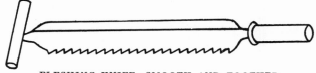

FLESHING KNIFE—SMOOTH AND TOOTHED

be made with a double edge. A rough serrated edge is sometimes useful in fleshing, and one edge of the fleshing knife may be filed into small teeth. A fleshing knife should not have a sharp edge, one at a right angle is better; in fact, a skate blade is quite successfully used sometimes.

The tanner uses a flesher by pushing it from him, as in that way he can control it much better, and the hide can be held from slipping by pressing a margin of it against the beam. Un-hairing, fleshing, sleeking and stretching are all done in this manner, as is also skiving or thinning down skins tanned for furs.

METHODS OF USING FLESHER ON BEAM

For unhairing tender skins like sheep or goat a knife of hardwood is perhaps better than metal, as it will be less likely to damage the grain. The Indians used wood or bone fleshers usually in making their buckskin.

The skiving or paring knife has the same general shape, but works quite differently as it is ground to a rather long bevel, like the

edge of a chisel, and then this thin edge is turned
over at right angles, making a short scraping

SKIVING OR PARING KNIFE

edge the whole
length of the
knife. A tool
called a turn-
ing steel
comes with such knives, as does also a smaller
one, the finger steel, for frequent dressing of
the turned edge. This skiving knife is used
chiefly by fur dressers and is quite expensive.
The leather maker will seldom need it, as it is
not often desirable for him to reduce a hide to
the same thickness all over. If a skin is to be
used as a robe or coat or in some cases small
skins for leather may need thinning in the neck
or back. A careful operator can do considerable
of this with a sharp draw knife or a steel cabinet
scraper can be ground and turned sufficiently to
do a little thinning down. A long sharp butcher
knife also can be used for thinning with great
care.

The handles of slickers with inserted blades
of copper, brass, etc., is a matter of individual
taste. Something to fill the hands when pushing

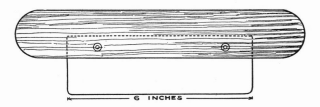

SLICKER OR SLEEKER
Brass, Copper or Slate Edge, set in Wooden Handle.

them over the hides. Some have a long blade, curved to fit the beam, and with a handle at each

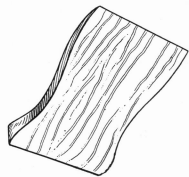

A WOODEN SLICKER, WEDGE SHAPED

end. Wooden slickers are very good and if made of hickory and other hard-wood will last for considerable time. A very good size is six inch blade and shaped as illustration, which is about an inch in thickness at widest end and some ten inches long.

A dull hatchet can be used (if it is smooth by rounding on edge) so as not to scratch the grain. A dull ax head held in a vise makes a

good stake for softening skins, only all iron
tools rust so quickly they have to be cleaned and
oiled every time they are used, and even then

HATCHET HEAD AND WALL PAPER SCRAPER
Used as Emergency Slickers (left); Ax Head, good shape; for
Emergency Stake—Fasten in Vice.

may stain the leather. Hard wood is to be preferred—such as the wedge shape wooden slicker
shown.

TWO HANDLED SCUDDING KNIFE
Used like Slicker, curved to fit beam. Brass, copper or slate edge, to
avoid rust.

Slickers or sleeking knives are made of copper, brass, slate or wood, seldom steel, as the

edges are rounded. They may be made by mounting a piece of the material about one-fourth inch thick, six inches long and four inches wide in a wooden handle. One long edge is secured in the handle and the other smoothly rounded is used to work over both surfaces of the leather by pushing hard against them and away from the operator.

The stake or stake knife can be also made of

STAKE KNIFE
For "Breaking" Skins

hard wood from a piece of board one inch thick, six inches wide and t w o and one-half or three feet long. The top end of this board is shaved to a wedge shape not more than one-eighth inch thick at the edge and with nicely rounded corners. This should be fastened upright either to a post or a movable plank base, well braced. Sometimes the working edge is made of metal and sometimes it is mounted on a crutch shaped handle and is called a shoulder stake. The stake knives are used in

breaking up and softening tanned hides.   **In**
doing this the hide is pulled back and forth over
the stake is in polishing shoes, but in using the
shoulder stake one side of the hide is held in a
clamp, and the other in the left hand, while the
right hand holds and guides the stake knife,
pressed against the hide by the operator's
shoulder.

Tanning is essentially rather dirty work; an
overall job in every way, and especially hard on
shoes, as they are subject to chemical slop and
drip always.   Some of the chrome solutions are
somewhat poisonous to the hands if they are
wet with them for long periods.   This is seldom
necessary, however, and good rinsing after such
immersion in chrome liquids is usually sufficient
to prevent bad effects.   Of course salt and lime
solutions always find their way into any cuts or
scratches on the hands, but the results are not
serious.

If bark is to be used some form of mill is
almost a necessity, as to cut up by hand the
quantity required will be a very tedious per-
formance.   There are a number of small hand
mills, sold chiefly for grinding poultry feed,

which may be adjusted to grind bark if it is well dried and chopped up coarsely with a hatchet first. In order to extract the tannin properly bark should not be coarser than grains of corn.

We have endeavored to speak only of such hand tools as are practically indispensable. The modern tannery is filled with machinery adapted to nearly all processes, from the soaking to finishing the leather.

SHOULDER STAKE MADE FROM CHOPPING KNIFE
(Back Ground Calf Leather, Home Tanned)

PRACTICE SKINS, DOG AND SQUIRREL, HAIR ON
(Tanned)

PRACTICE SKINS (RAW), WOODCHUCK OR GROUND
HOG AND SQUIRREL

CHAPTER IV

MATERIALS

IRST and foremost we must have a plentiful supply of clean, soft water. If water from wells, springs or streams contains more than a trace of mineral, rain water should be used.

TEST FOR HARD WATER: Take a piece of common cheap bar soap and a dish of cold water; wash the hands in it, using plenty of soap; if it curdles it is unfit for tanning.

All real leather is freed from hair, and for this lime is the tanner's standby. Use only good burned or caustic lime free from dirt and stone. This can be made by burning lime stone or, lacking that, the shells of shellfish in the usual way. Fresh hydrated lime may be used instead of slacking burnt lime. Air slacked lime is of no use.

Lye is used sometimes alone or combined with lime for unhairing skins and in making a soap useful in softening tanned hides. It may be had at grocery stores in the form of a salt (potash salts), or we can make it as the pioneers did from hardwood ashes. To do this prepare an ash hopper or leach. This can be made of a section of hollow log or a barrel with both heads knocked out. Cut a series of notches around the bottom (or bore a number of inch holes) and stand it on a piece of wide plank. This plank should be raised from the ground enough

to set a bucket under it and have a half inch groove cut in it around the bottom of barrel to lead the lye to one side. Make this side of shelf or bench a little lower so as to d r a i n the leaching to that point where it can drip into a bucket. Put a layer

BARREL OR ASH LEACH

of little sticks in the bottom of barrel, cover with an inch or two of straw or coarse grass and put the ashes in. Make a basin-shaped depression in the top of the ashes and pour a bucket of rain water in. In a few hours the lye will begin to trickle through.

From time to time add water as it runs through. If the ashes are well tamped it will trickle through slowly. That is what you want. The first run of lye should be strong enough to float an egg; if it fails to do so, put it through again or boil it down. A rough and ready way to procure a small amount of lye is to boil hardwood ashes in soft water, allow them to settle and pour off the clear part. Save this and repeat until a quantity of weak lyes have accumulated, then boil it down until strong enough.

To make soft soap, put twelve quarts of lye in a bucket or pot, bring to a boil and add to it meat rinds, fat or any kind of animal grease to make it as thick as porridge when cold. Let it boil two hours before cooling a sample to try it. The addition of salt and rosin will make common hard soap, but the soft variety is most useful in tanning. Get unsalted grease if you can, as a tanned skin should be free from salt or it will draw moisture from the air in damp weather and feel slimy. The manufactured lye has directions with it for making both hard and soft soap.

The making of potash was at one time a backwoods industry, indulged in between seasons by hunters and trappers of small capital but plentiful muscle. An ax and large iron pot made all the needful equipment, as with these, acres of hardwoods were felled, burned, the ashes leached and the lye evaporated, until a barrel or so of potash salts was obtained. This loaded aboard a canoe or raft was floated a few hundred miles and sold for a small amount of real money or bartered for powder, lead, salt or hardware.

Salt is also one of the prime necessities when handling hides or tanning. The coarsely ground grade is all right for large and heavy hides, but fine salt is best for skins and making solutions. It comes in 100 lb. sacks and smaller containers. When salted hides are dry enough to become hard, the surplus may be shaken off and gathered up for further use if not too bloody or dirty. Use this for the first salting.

Barks and leaves containing enough tannin acid to be useful are to be gathered in many places. Hemlock bark and that of several species of oak are most commonly used, and the leaves of the common sumac are in some demand for both tanning and dying leather. Barks are usually gathered while the sap is up, as they can be peeled most readily then. They should be stacked or piled to dry and afterward stored under sheds until used. Before using, cut or grind fairly fine.

Animal fats and grease should be rendered, before using to soften hides. When used without rendering or heating they "burn," or rather oxidize in contact with the air and destroy the hide fibre finally. This way raw skins left long with an adhering coat of fat become rotten or "grease burnt," especially if the weather is warm.

Chemicals should be of good quality and fresh and clean, if possible. When stale or weak, larger amounts will be required, and unless a chemist the worker will hardly know just what proportions to use. What is known as the commercial grade or tanner's chemicals will do the work, but will probably require larger quantities than the U. S. P. or highest grade. Of course these should be procured before they are needed and may be kept on hand for some time when handled right. Keep in glass or earthen jars with tight covers of the same material, in a dry place. Dealers in tanner's supplies keep these, or they may be had from local druggists in small amounts generally, but if they do not handle them, they can give the address of some manufacturing chemist who does.

Chrome Alum or Chromium Potassium Sulphate crystals furnish the active agent in making chrome leather and should be in the form of dark, hard, glossy, plum-colored crystals. The lighter, crumbly, dull ones are not so desirable. Sodium Carbonate crystals or Washing Soda also ought to be clear and glass like. The crusted, partly air slacked lumps are inferior.

Common Alum, Ammonium or Potash Alum is used much in tanning light skins and lace leather. Liquid Sulphuric Acid, sometimes called Oil of Vitriol, may be the commercial quality. Be careful in keeping it in bottles as it burns the cork in a short time. Oxalic Acid is used in the form of pulverized crystals, a much milder acid than the Sulphuric; it is also used to remove blood stains, clean straw hats, etc. Lactic Acid is a mild acid, present in sour milk.

Vinegar, a diluted form of Acetic Acid is used as a substitute for Lactic Acid to neutralize lime solutions in hides.

There are a great number of other chemicals which may be used in tanning to help remove the glue and separate and toughen the fibres, but some of the processes are quite complicated and others too expensive for general use.

Oils and greases play an important part in softening and lubricating skin fibres. Almost any such material of animal origin is useful to the tanner. Sometimes he can use mineral oil (some of the coal oil products), but vegetable oils never. Clean, unsalted, rendered animal fat or grease, such as is produced from lard and tallow, and oil from various fish is used contantly. Beeswax is combined with grease to fill leather to make it waterproof. Petrolatum · vaseline and paraffin wax are also compo- nts of such filling or "dubbing."

CHAPTER V

METHODS AND TERMS

EATHER making or tanning is any process of preparing animal skins which converts the raw skin, subject to putrefaction into insoluble material of strength and pliability. In order to make plain the wherefor of different manipulations a word as to hide structure will be well.

A hide or skin is not a single piece of the same material throughout like a board, but consists of three principal layers, the epidermis on the outside, then the true fibrous skin or derma which forms the leather, and an inner muscular

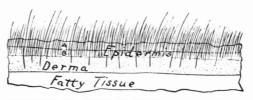

SECTION OF SKIN OR HIDE. (MAGNIFIED)

layer connecting the whole, to the flesh and muscles of the carcass. A raw animal skin decays rapidly if kept subject to heat and moisture; if dried it becomes stiff and hard, or it may be converted into glue by boiling.

Tanning changes this and gives us a material, porous, flexible, and of great durability. By various means, (the use of some form of tannic acid generally), the glue is removed and the skin fibres separated from each other and toughened. By working oil or grease of some kind into the open pores of the leather while drying, a more or less flexible state is attained. Tanned leathers are dyed or colored to suit the taste or styles and sometimes polished also.

In making leather, both the inner muscular tissue and the epidermis with its accompanying hair or wool are removed, leaving only the fibrous derma. Fur skin dressing differs chiefly in the preservation entire (if possible) of the coat of epidermis and hair. So though many of the processes are similar, fur dressing is sometimes called tawing to distinguish it from leather tanning.

The making of buckskin is not tanning, but a softening of the skin by mechanical means, motion, etc., and does not produce a material as moisture resisting and desirable as when regularly tanned.

Divided according to the materials used there are, roughly speaking, four principal modes of tanning:

1. Vegetable Tanning.
2. Chemical or Mineral Tanning.
3. Combination Tanning.
4. Oil Tanning.

1. VEGETABLE TANNING by the use of tannic acid contained in barks, leaves, wood, etc. Much heavy leather like harness and sole is produced so, but it requires the maximum amount of time; a number of months in some cases.

2. MINERAL OR CHEMICAL TANNING with various salts and acids. Nearly all fur skins are tanned by some of these preparations, as they do not stain or discolor the fur and a comparatively short time is necessary.

3. COMBINATION TANNING. Both chemicals and vegetable tannins are used in these processes, which are more rapid than when vegetable tannins are used exclusively. Chrome leather is produced by both the Chemical and Combination methods.

4. OIL TANNING. Indian buckskin making resembles in some degree Oil Tanning, as is the

making of chamois leather (from sheep). In chamoising the skins are subject to warmth while filled with some form of oil or grease and the resulting chemical action forms an acid in the leather itself which produces the desired result. The action of natural grease left on a skin is something like this, only in such a case the grease is usually left in the skin so long that the oxidizing process affects the skin fibres too severely.

About five operations are necessary in tanning, (without counting the frequent washings) in the following order:

PROCESS 1. SOAKING: To render hides flexible and to clean all hides of dirt, salt, blood, etc.

PROCESS 2. UNHAIRING: By the use of a lime solution usually, sometimes by sweating or heat and moisture, also by lye or potash alone or combined with lime.

PROCESS 3. DELIMING: Removing the alkali which would interfere with or neutralize the action of tannin (an acid). This is accomplished by either of two methods. Soaking with a weak acid or fermenting with animal or vegetable bacteria.

PROCESS 4. TANNING PROPER: Py immersion in one or more vegetable or chemical solutions until fully penetrated. This is what alters the entire nature of the hide and when completed warmth, moisture and even boiling will change it but little.

PROCESS 5. FINISHING: Consists of currying, or softening the tanned hide by working, rolling, etc., to separate the drying fibres, at the same time forcing oils or grease into the pores to lubricate and retain such flexibility as is needed. At this stage also the coloring is done, as much leather is white or nearly so, though some vegetable tannins give it a light brown or tan color. A glaze or hard, shiny surface is added for patent and similar finishes.

Like any other business tanning has a number of technical terms and special names descriptive in most cases, but not always clear to those not in the know. Some of the commonest are given below:

FLESHING: Scraping the flesh sides to remove the inner muscular coat as well as adhering bits of flesh and fat. This exposes the true fibrous skin to chemical action.

GRAINING: Unhairing, removing the hair or wool, together with the grain or epidermis from skins that are made into leather.

LIMING: Soaking in lime solution to loosen the hair and grain.

SLEEKING OR STRIKING OUT OR SCUDDING: Working liquids out of skins by pressure and scraping.

PICKLING OR TANNING: Soaking in the various tanning solutions.

SKIVING: Thinning tanned skins by paring.

BATING: Removing lime by fermentation.

SCOURING: Washing to clean skins.

SAMMING: Partly drying.

HANDLING OR PADDLING: Stirring or working skins about in the various solutions.

STRETCHING OR BREAKING: Separating the fibres of partly dried skins by mechanical means.

STAKING: Using a tool called the stake knife in breaking or softening.

BOWLING: Rolling tanned skins on a table to soften and work oil into them.

PLUNGING: Working sides or strips up and

down about in the liquids so as to expose all parts to the action of fresh solution.

DRENCHING: Freeing limed hides of the lime (alkali) by washing in an acid liquid.

NEUTRALIZING: The reverse of the above process. Washing in an alkalin solution in order to stop the action of acid in skins sufficiently tanned.

DAMPING BACK: To re-soften by moisture a tanned skin which has bceome dry before being sufficiently softened.

Fur skins, while not requiring any treatment to rid them of hair and grain, must go through several additional operations to free them of grease and dirt and dry the fur light and fluffy.

CHAPTER VI

 GREEN hide may be started in process as soon as it has cooled from the animal heat after taking off. To leave it spread out eight or ten hours, or over night will be long enough. If the hide has been salted, shake well to remove most of the salt, then while spread out, hair side down, trim off the tail, head back of the ears, shanks, and all ragged edges and tag ends. Put the trimmed hide, hair side up, on the beam or table and using a sharp knife split from neck to tail down the back, making what is called two "sides." In the case of large hides it will be found more convenient for handling to split each side lengthwise through the "break" just above the flank, making of it four strips, the strip next the back bone being about twice as wide as the thinner belly strip. This way a hide will furnish two sides or four strips which may be tanned alike or the heaviest back strips made into sole leather and the others in strap, harness or lace as may be wanted.

In speaking of sides in handling it is understood to be sides or strips as the case may be.

After splitting the hide, fill one of your barrels with clean, cool water and suspend the sides in it by hanging flesh side out over the sticks prepared for this purpose. Let them soak about three hours, stirring about often to loosen and wash out blood, dirt and salt. Now take out the sides or strips one at a time and laying on the beam hair side up, scrub well with a stiff brush to remove all dirt and manure, and when all have been so treated wash well in a tub of clean water. Then put the strips on the beam flesh side up, and with a sharp butcher knife, draw knife or flesher cut off any pieces of meat that may be sticking to it.

After this, go over the entire flesh side with a dull flesher or the back of butcher or draw knife, holding the knife by both ends and pushing it away from you hard against the hide. You can hold the hide in place by letting a margin of it hang over the end of the beam and pressing against it with the body. Thus it can be easily moved about until all parts are gone

MOVEABLE AND ADJUSTABLE BEAM FOR SMALL
HIDES
A Broad Flesher stuck in end of Beam.

over. Do not neglect this working over, as it helps open up and soften the hide.

Rinse off again in clean water, refill the soak barrel with clean, cool water, and hang the hides in it as before; plunge and stir them about at intervals until they are soft and flexible, which should be in from twelve to twenty-four hours for a green hide and twenty-four to forty-eight hours for a green salted hide. Of course dry salted and flint hides require still longer to relax. A low temperature will also lengthen the time of soaking.

Hides should be soft and clean all over before putting in the lime. Flint dry hides will require several alternate scrapings and soakings, as a tough glazed surface will be found on the flesh side which must be cut and scraped away in order to allow penetration by any liquid. A toothed flesher is good to help break this glaze, and it will require repeated applications of it backed by some force to get the hide sufficiently soft.

When it is about like a freshly removed skin, put on the beam again and give the flesh side another working over, even though there seems to be little or nothing to remove, as such working out is necessary to properly open the pores of the hide so it may take the tan properly.

After this wash off again clean. It is now ready for liming. When hydrated lime is used, all that is necessary is to stir about eight pounds of it into nearly a barrel of water, (the soak barrel will do after washing it out) and it is ready for hanging the sides or strips in. When using burnt or caustic lime this preparation should begin the day the skin was first put to soak. To prepare lime for a single large or medium hide, put five pounds of burnt lime in a clean wooden tub with about a quart of water and as the lime begins to slake add more water, a little at a time, enough to prevent it getting dry but not enough to quench the slaking. When it seems to be all slaked stir in one or two more gallons of water just as when making whitewash, and cover with boards or sacks until the hide is ready.

When this stage is reached pour the slaked lime into a clean barrel, add enough water to nearly fill and stir it up. See to it that hides are so hung that they are completely covered by the lime water and have as few folds and wrinkles as possible. Keep the barrel covered, except when you stir the lime water and plunge the hides three or four times a day until the hair will come out easily. Early in the liming it will be possible to *pull* the hair out, but this is not sufficient; by *easily* we mean until it will come off by rubbing over with the hand. This will require from six to ten days in warm weather and possibly as long as sixteen days in winter.

CHAPTER VII

UNHAIRING AND DELIMING

O TEST the liming, throw the sides on the beam, hair up, and with a dull flesher, the back of a knife, or even a piece of square edged iron bar, held nearly flat against the hide, push off the hair, together with a cheesy layer of the skin. The latter, the grain or epidermis, is usually a darker color than the true skin underneath, so it is easy to see when it has been removed. If this does not rub off readily, return to the lime until it does.

If any fine hairs seem to remain after un-hairing, put back in the lime another day so they may be easily scraped off. When completely unhaired, "scud" out all the lime, grease and dirt you can by working over the grain side with a dull knife or slicker. Use a considerable force and a tool with rounded edge to avoid scratching the grain.

When this side has been completely worked over, turn over and work over the flesh side with a fleshing knife, making sure of the removal of *all* bits of flesh and the entire inner muscular coating of the hide. When the skin is thick you can use a very sharp knife, either butcher or draw knife, with a slight drawing motion, something as in shaving the face. It needs considerable practice to do this without cutting holes in the hide, though.

Next, wash both sides of the hide with scrubbing brush and clean water, then put in clean, cool water for about six hours, washing well and changing the water four or five times. After this is completed, deliming or drenching is necessary to prepare the hide for tanning. Its principal object is to remove the lime from the hide, as its presence would neutralize and render ineffective the vegetable or chemical acids used to tan the hide fibre. At one time this was most frequently done by fermenting with animal bacteria, but a weak acid drench is so much simpler and above all cleaner, that we recommend its use exclusively.

Prepare the drenching or deliming liquor by nearly filling a clean barrel with clean, cool water, to which add three ounces (fluid ounces) of lactic acid.   If you cannot get the U. S. P. grade use about three times as much tanner's lactic acid, or one-half gallon of good sharp vinegar.   Lactic acid produces the best results and is to be preferred for this purpose.   Stir this acid solution well and hang the sides in it for twenty-four hours, plunging them up and down and stirring the liquor occasionally.

After removing from the acid drench work over or scud both sides of the hide as was done after liming to work out the solution and open the pores of skin that they may receive the tanning solution.   For heavy hides producing sole, belting and harness leather hang in a barrel of cool water over night, rinse off and proceed to tanning.   Small skins for thin, soft leather do not need the over night soaking, but may be put to tan at once after rinsing thoroughly with several changes of water.

The lime water sludge and fleshings from the liming may be safely emptied in fields or garden, as it has some fertilizing value, particularly on acid soils.   The hair, after being scraped off may be collected separately, rinsed and dried and put aside for several purposes.   While this is hardly worth while with only a hide or two, if saved a sufficient quantity to be useful will soon accumulate.

The hides are now ready for actual tanning process. All hides tanned as leather should undergo similar preliminary work, that is, soaking, fleshing, liming, unhairing and deliming with the frequent working over, washing out and rinsing. Such treatment will require from one to three weeks to complete; not that amount of actual working time, of course, but that length of time will be needed for the processes. In warm weather and on fresh hides a single week may be enough, while dry skins and winter temperature will call for three or four times as long.

CHAPTER VIII

TANNING

ANNING follows after deliming and varies in detail according to the material used. This should be procured and prepared beforehand so the tanning may proceed without loss of time.

See that barrels are clean before putting tanning solutions in. Hang skins on sticks as was done in soaking and liming and keep as free as possible of folds and wrinkles, that all parts may be affected equally. Plunge tanning skins up and down and stir the solution frequently, as when they remain quiet that part of the solution in immediate contact with the skin becomes weakened and has less effect. Moving about brings fresh and stronger solution in contact and lessens the time of tanning. In large tanneries where power is available the vats are agitated constantly greatly shortening the time of this process. If the hand worker will bear this in mind and can locate the tan barrel where other work takes him near it at intervals, stirring it at such times will help matters.

As to when tanning is complete, small and light skins are said to be done when on pinching up a fold a white line is produced which remains on flattening out the fold. A more certain test is to cut a small piece from the thickest part of the hide (the neck) and examine the freshly cut edge. If it seems to be evenly colored all through, the tanning is about done. If, however, the outside color seems to extend only part way through, it should be kept in the tan longer. The surest test is to boil the small piece cut off, in water, a few minutes; if it curls up and becomes hard or rubbery it is not done, and the skins should be left in until a small piece is changed but little by boiling. When tanning is complete the hides are removed and washed in clear water, after some processes and in chemical solutions after others.

In the tanning formulas given in the following chapters, the proper washing solutions are given. This washing should be thorough, especially after acid processes, as it is necessary to wash out or neutralize any acid remaining in the hides, which if left would continue acting and finally weaken the fibre of the leather.

Neglect in this respect has made many handlers of skins prejudiced against such processes, when in reality they are great time savers, much cleaner than some of the old processes, and in the case of fur dressing help to prevent damage by insects. The acid, like fire, is a good servant when well controlled. Fire will clear out underbrush nicely, but unless stopped will grow and destroy the standing timber; so acid helps remove first that part of the skin not needed for leather, and then if not stopped will attack the useful fibre.

As a general thing the amounts of tanning solution given as proper will be about exhausted by tanning the indicated amount of hides, though a few small skins may perhaps be tanned with it by allowing rather longer time and fortifying it with some fresh solution. Generally it will be as well to dump out spent tan and some care should be taken to dispose of it where farm animals will not drink it, as although not poisonous to handle, it would if taken internally probably be fatal. It also has a bad effect on the soil, killing most vegetation it comes in contact with.

To re-tan skins that have not been sufficiently processed is rather difficult and unsatisfactory, as we can seldom tell just what has been done or not done to them. Thorough soaking out and close watching in the tan may bring them around.

After tanning and washing out, the next step is drying out unless it is desired to color the leather. Never dry out sides or strips in the sun or near heat. A shady, not too airy place is best. Do not let them dry out without oiling while still damp.

The difference in time required to make leather is chiefly due to the slow or quick action of the tanning solutions. This varies from two or three days' immersion in acid solution for light skins, to as much as seven and a half months in bark solution required for sole leather.

For emergency work some form of chemical tanning is to be selected, as by its use we can produce leather and make use of it, if not use it up, before it could be finished by the slower bark process. There are so many vegetable substances containing tannin in varying amounts and of different degrees of solubility which should be used, and if one has time for experiments might be interesting to try out. In Europe the acorns and acorn cups of a certain variety of oak are much used, and probably some of our native oaks would furnish something almost equally good. This book, however, has no space for what has not been tested, as the processes detailed here have been.

LEATHER FROM AN IMPROPERLY SKINNED HIDE

This leather is unfit for many purposes because of damage from numerous scores (wavy lines) and cuts (black lines and holes).

CHAPTER IX

SOFTENING AND FINISHING

HIS is at once a very important and also laborious part of tanning. A part of the softening is accomplished by oiling, but all oil or grease applied should be worked into the leather. Such rubbing, rolling and bending works the oil into the pores and lubricate the fibres so they slide over each other. All softening processes begin when the tanned skins are partly dry and are continued until they are fully dry and sufficiently flexible. They should be at least slightly damp at first and the oiling and working continued until dry.

Sole leather, of course, is not worked up soft but kept flat and dressed with heavier grease. Light leathers and skins for robe or garment use must be perfectly soft and require much working over. Some of this is done on the "stake knife" or floor stake described heretofore by pulling back and forth over it, flesh side next the knife as a cloth is used in shining shoes.

FLOOR STAKE IN CENTER; WASHING TUB AND PIECE OF HOME TANNED
LEATHER AT RIGHT; SOLUTION BARREL (SMALL) DRAW KNIFE
AND SHOULDER STAKE (LEFT)

Another way is to make a pad of several layers of old blanket, quilt or similar things, and put it on the beam with the skin over it flesh side up. Then stretch it well in all directions by pushing with a dull flesher. In some cases the pad may be put on the table top and a shoulder stake used to do the stretching.

Bowling or rolling the oiled skin up and then rolling on the table with the hands with considerable pressure is another mode of softening. A square edged bar of iron secured in a vise may be used, pulling the partly dry skin back and forth around it. Skins should be well worked up once before oiling, then rolled up and left a while to allow the oil or grease to penetrate and worked again.

If neither bark or gum catechu are used the leather will be practically white unless dyed. This should be done after tanning, neutralizing and washing and before applying oil dressings to the leather. The simplest mode of dyeing leather black is by the use of a preparation known as Nigrosine. One-half ounce water-soluble Nigrosine dissolved in one and one-fourth pints water is the correct proportion.

Mix a sufficient quantity of this and apply with a brush to the damp hides, then proceed with oiling and finishing.

A fairly good black may be had by application of iron liquor and sumac solution. Iron liquor is made by putting clear iron filings in one-half gallon of sharp vinegar and letting it stand a few days. Add enough filings from time to time so there will always be some undissolved.

The sumac solution is made by crumbling ten or fifteen pounds of dried sumac leaves into a barrel containing thirty-five or forty gallons of warm water. Stir it well and when cool hang the sides or strips in it for about two days. Plunge and stir them about frequently and on taking out rinse off any particles of leaves, drain a few minutes and brush over with the iron liquor. Rinse off any excess and put back in the sumac over night. If not sufficiently black next morning, repeat the brushing with iron liquor and return to the sumac twelve hours more. On finally removing from the sumac rinse well, scrub with warm water and last of all wash for some hours with several changes of water.

There are a number of older methods of coloring with preparations of logwood and copperas, but if possible get the water-soluble nigrosine; it is to be preferred, as they and also the iron and sumac are somewhat troublesome and sometimes injure the grain of the leather.

Let the wet leather dry out slowly after the neutralizing, washing or dyeing, as the case may be.

To finish sole leather, after tanning and rinsing lay the sides or strips down and press out most of the water by covering with some old dry cloths and treading over the whole surface, then hang up until they are only damp. While still damp give them a good coat of oil on the grain side only, and hang up again until fully dry.

Sole leather should be waterproofed by greasing heavily, and especially that made by the chrome process. Such waterproofing is best done after the shoes are repaired by setting them in a shallow dish of warm grease or oil of such depth as to just cover the soles. Such grease should not be used hotter than the hand can bear and any surplus wiped off when cool.

There are several formulas for such grease; plain melted paraffine wax will answer but will make the shoe soles stiff. A good mixture is:

Vaseline, by weight..................8 parts
Beeswax ....1 part

Another:

Tallow ....3 parts
Oil, fish or neatsfoot................1 part

Harness and belting leather are finished in a slightly different way. Take it when still quite damp after the tan and rinsing water have been pressed out, slick over the grain side thoroughly and give it a liberal coat of neatsfoot or fish oil. Hang up, or better, tack out, spread smooth and let dry *slowly*. When dry damped back by wetting or rolling up in wet burlap until damp and limber all over. Prepare a stuffing or "dubbing" of equal parts tallow and neatsfoot oil or fish oil and tallow. These should be melted together and when cool be soft and pasty but not liquid. Add more tallow if the mixture is too thin. Apply a thin coating of this to the grain side while it is warm and hang them up to dry. When dry remove the surplus stuffing by working over the grain side with the slicker. If there is not enough grease in the leather yet, dampen back again and repeat the process of greasing, drying and slicking. Finally rub over with sawdust to remove a surplus of the grease.

Thin leathers are finished by oiling the damp leather, stretching out and drying, damping back, slicking, staking and drying. If one round of such treatment does not soften it enough, repeat it. Do not apply tallow or heavy grease to light skins and spend plenty of time slicking and staking it.

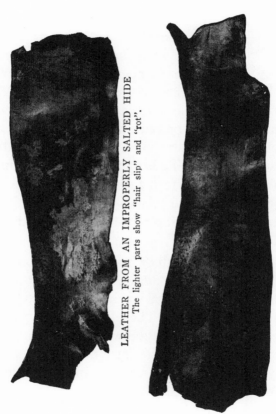

LEATHER FROM AN IMPROPERLY SALTED HIDE
The lighter parts show "hair slip" and "rot".

LEATHER FROM A GRUBBY HIDE
The grub holes appear as black specks near the middle and top.

CHAPTER X

OR this purpose select hides of from twenty to forty pounds weight, and put them through the preliminary treatment as laid out in Chapters VI and VII. While the strips are in the lactic acid or vinegar drench, prepare the alum solution in the following manner: Take a clean barrel, the one used for the liming is all right after washing out, and put in it fifteen gallons of water, clean and soft, and twelve pounds of ammonia alum or potash alum, stirring frequently until entirely dissolved.

Put in a wooden tub or bucket five gallons of clean cold water and add six pounds of clean salt and three pounds of washing soda (sodium carbonate) crystals. These should be bright and glasslike. The opaque white lumps are inferior. Dissolve by stirring; then very, very slowly pour the soda solution into the alum solution in the barrel, stirring constantly as you do. Take as much as ten minutes to pour the soda in, as if it is done much quicker it will turn milky and will not tan. Take the strips from the drench and after washing well, hang on sticks in the alum solution. Enough water should be added to nearly fill the barrel.

Plunge the strips and stir the alum solution six or eight times a day for six or seven days. Then remove from the alum-soda solution and wash well for fifteen minutes in clean, cold water. Put on clean boards to drain for half an hour, then hang up by one edge to dry, turning every hour, so that first one edge and then the other is up. Hang in a moderately warm place free from draughts and do not forget to turn them, as if one edge is left down it may get "cracky." If some parts dry out faster than others, use a wet rag or brush to moisten them so they may progress evenly. The edges and thinner places are especially liable to dry first. When the strips have become somewhat stiff, about as much so as a harness strap, and can be bent short without cracking but are still damp, begin to work them to soften them by staking vigorously. The floor stake is best for this purpose, used as indicated in Chapter IX.

The more time devoted to this part of the

business the more pliable the lace leather will be. As this leather is white it will look much better if kept clean during the softening process. After staking well, lay the sides or strips on the table, flesh side up, and work over them with a wooden slicker, which should have a very smooth edge. The grain sides also should have the same treatment, before oiling. Prepare the oil by melting together three pounds of tallow and one pint of neatsfoot oil. If neatsfoot is not to be had, cod or any fish oil or even a medium automobile cylinder oil can be substituted for it.

If the strips are not still soft and uniformly damp, wrap them in damp cloths or put in damp sawdust, until they are moist but not wet, all over. Then with a brush, apply a heavy coat of grease to both sides of the damp strips. The grease should be as hot as the hand can bear when applied and it should be done in a very warm place.

After greasing roll the strips together and keep for two or three days in a warm place. Unroll and stake thoroughly if not too dry. If too stiff and hard damp them back, with cloths or sawdust first. If the lace leather is not soft enough now, grease both sides, roll up and lay away for two days more. After this repeat the staking and working with the wooden slicker to work in and remove the excess of grease. The leather should be staked again, oiled with oil only this time, and staked and slicked until when thoroughly dried out it remains perfectly soft. Thorough staking when nearly dry is needed to produce this result.

There is quite a little art in cutting laces or thongs from a piece of leather in order to get them uniform. Short thongs are cut from the side of a piece by driving an awl or wire nail into a piece of board and beside it, just the width of the lace apart stick the blade of a sharp knife, inclined a little to the rear. After making a starting cut on the edge you can with a steady pull draw the cut strip between the knife and nail, thus getting a lace of uniform width.

Two short thongs may be easily spliced without knotting by cutting a short slit in the ends of each, and after slipping one slit end over the other, bring the other end of the outside thong up through the slit and pull to tighten.

To make a long thong without splices it is only necessary to cut out a circular or oval piece of leather, and using the knife with the nail gauge cut the entire piece spirally. In fact, an entire hide can be cut into a single thong if so wanted.

The entire time necessary to make lace leather by this process should be from fifteen to thirty days, depending on the temperature and the condition of the hides.

CHAPTER XI

CHROME PROCESS

HIS process is used in making both light and heavy leathers of a very durable quality in a comparatively short time. It is inclined to be rather stretchy, so before cutting up for use it is best to take most of the stretch out of it. Also when used for shoe soles it needs to be well filled with grease to waterproof it to some extent, as it is rather porous.

The use of chemicals, principally what is known as "chrome alum" give its name to the process by which a very satisfactory leather can be made in a few weeks, as against many months by the older method of bark tanning.

After selecting such a skin as is desirable, proceed with the soaking, cleaning, liming, etc., in the usual way until the skins are unhaired, then if for strap, upper and thin leathers put the limed skin into a tub of clean water. Water should be lukewarm but not too hot; never uncomfortably warm to the hand. Leave the skins in this four to eight hours, according to size Hides designed for sole, belting and harness leathers should be soaked in cool water only, for about six hours, changing the water four or five times meanwhile.

For any large hides make the drench the regular strength. Three ounces lactic acid to about forty gallons or a barrel of water. But for light skins, under fifteen pounds weight each, use one-third less acid or about two ounces to same quantity water. These smaller skins should be simply rinsed off with water after working over from the drench, while heavier hides for sole, belting and harness stock should be hung in a barrel of cool water over night before putting them in to tan.

Make up the chrome tanning solution at least two days before it is to be used; not in any case later than when the hide is taken from the lime. Do not throw the ingredients together by guess, but weigh the chemicals and measure the water carefully. A good way to measure the water is to measure say two gallons with a small measure into a bucket and mark the exact place, then use the buckets in filling barrels and tubs

The chemicals required, common salt, washing soda, crystals and chrome alum should be clean and of good quality. If you cannot get U. S. P. quality, different amounts will be required, depending of course on the strength of the materials offered, and only a chemist could give the proper quantity.

For each hide of over thirty pounds weight use three and one-half pounds soda crystals and six pounds salt, dissolved in three gallons of warm water, in a wooden tub or bucket. Also put twelve pounds chrome alum in a half barrel or large tub with nine gallons of cool water and stir frequently until dissolved, which will take some time. Use a wooden paddle for stirring, and when you are sure by feeling around with it in the bottoms of the tubs that the chemicals are fully dissolved, pour the soda and salt solution into the chrome alum solution. Pour very slowly, stirring the mixture constantly. Take at least ten minutes to pour the soda solution in. As a result there will be about twelve gallons of what is called the "stock chrome solution," which should be kept in a wooden tub or half barrel well covered.

To start tanning, put about thirty gallons of cool water in a clean barrel and add four gallons of the chrome solution, mixing well by stirring. In this suspend the sides or strips on sticks and plunge and stir frequently for three days. At the end of three days remove the sides, while four gallons more of the stock solution are added to and mixed with that already in the tan barrel. Hang the sides back in the re-enforced tan liquor and plunge and stir them three or four times each day for three days or more. At the end of this time, remove the sides again while the tan is fortified once more with the remaining four gallons of the stock solution. Stir and move about as before for about four days, when the tanning should be complete. Cut a little piece from the thickest part and if it seems to be colored evenly a bluish or greenish all the way through it is probably done, but to make sure apply the boiling test.

When the tanning is done, take the sides out and put them in a barrel of clean water where they should be well washed, changing the water about four times. Prepare a neutralizing bath by dissolving two pounds of borax in forty gallons of water and soak the hides in this twelve hours, or over night, plunging and stirring about frequently. After this soaking in borax to neutralize, take out and wash for an entire day with five or six changes of water. Remove from this and drain, and the hides are ready to dye if you wish to color them, and if not, proceed with oiling and finishing.

You will remember that the actual time in the tan for this process is about ten days. Of course the preliminary work and the finishing are nearly the same in all the processes thus indicating a gain of over four months in making leather, over the old style bark process.

Also it is almost impossible to prepare bark properly without a mill of some kind, as a single hide calls for about twice its weight in bark.

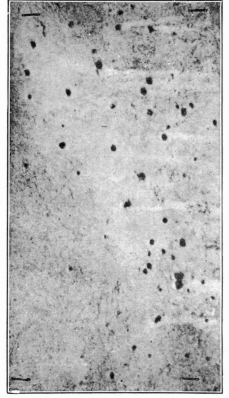

LEATHER FROM A HEAVY, GRUBBY HIDE
Grubby leather is unfit for good outsoles, shoe uppers, harness or belting.

CHAPTER XII

ACID PROCESS

THIS is another mode of tanning which requires comparatively little time, yet when properly carried out produces a very good grade of leather. When used as a strictly acid process it seems best adapted to light weight skins. Fur skin dressers in particular make much use of it.

There are a number of acids in use for this purpose, but we will give two formulas which seem to be as good as any. In one the agent is a crystalized salt, oxalic acid and the other sulphuric, a liquid.

If the skin is to be tanned as naked leather it should be put through the usual routine, liming to loosen the hair, and after removing it, drenching, to neutralize the alkali and washing out thoroughly before it is ready for the acid solution. To make enough of this to use in a half barrel will require about twenty gallons, leaving room for skins. This would answer for about ten light calf skins or any combination of skins totaling the same weight. Heat the water and dissolve in it one quart of salt to each gallon. Allow to cool before putting in the sulphuric acid. This is a fuming liquid which must not be allowed to come in contact with flesh, clothes or hides before being diluted. The bottle or jug in which it is kept should have a stopper of glass or something similar, as a cork is soon burned out. To measure it out procure a graduated measuring glass such as a druggist or photographer uses. Using this add one fluid ounce of acid for each gallon of water and stir the whole well. Do not lean over the tub and inhale the fumes while doing this. The skins may now be put in and stirred about from time to time until tanned. **Thin skins** will hardly require more than two days; thicker ones a week or more. The lower the temperature the slower the action of the pickle will be.

When you think it should be finished, test by cutting a bit from the neck and if so, neutralize by soaking two hours in a solution of washing soda. This should have at least one ounce or one and a half ounces to the gallon of water and after stirring and working about in it, wring out and rinse in clear water. Then hang up and allow to nearly dry. This treatment produces white leather, but if black is wanted it should be colored now before oiling; if not proceed to oil and break up to soften.

The preliminary work to the oxalic acid process is practically the same, and the·solution is made up in the following proportions:

To each gallon of water add two ounces by weight of pulverized oxalic acid and one pint of salt. Dissolve well before immersing the skins. Make up about two or three gallons for each skin the size of a sheep or calf. Very light skins may tan in this in one day or less; larger ones as calf or sheep will require two days or more. This makes a pure white leather very open and porous. For heavier leather or that which will be exposed to the weather, add to each gallon of the oxalic solution, six ounces of gum catechu, dissolved in hot water. This will also give the finished leather a tan color. More time should be given in this solution, ten days or more in some cases.

Oxalic acid is a poison taken internally, but this solution will not injure the hands. The sulphuric solution may make the hands smart but will do them no real harm. These acid pickles *must be* neutralized and well washed out or the leather will deteriorate and drop to pieces in a short time.

The oxalic without the gum catechu and the sulphuric solution are both adapted to tanning with hair or wool on, as the acids tend to clean the hair or fur and act as a moth preventive. In furs it is no disadvantage to have a very soft and porous leather.

CHAPTER XIII

THIS is one of the oldest methods of leather making and one in almost universal use, but one which requires a great deal of time to produce an excellent quality of leather when properly carried out. It is not often applied to the tanning of skins on which the hair or fur is to remain, however, as the material used is apt to stain or discolor the fur. The woodlands in nearly all parts of the country supply barks containing more or less amounts of tannic acid but the process is much less used than formerly, as other methods make for greater economy in time. No leather is better than good bark tanned and no other processes require as many months to produce it.

The bark most commonly used is that of hemlock, Spanish chestnut, Jack red, and in fact almost any of the oaks. Sumac leaves, some species of willow and even the tea leaves contain enough tannin for very small skins. I have heard of alfalfa being used as a substitute for bark in tanning.

The same work of preparation for actual tanning is gone through with as for other leather making, but at least fifteen or twenty days before we are ready to hang the hides into tan, the bark solution should be started by putting thirty or forty pounds of finely ground bark in a half barrel and pouring twenty gallons of boiling water over it. Bark should be ground quite fine to get good results; chopped into coarse pieces will not do. Use only rain or other soft water and keep covered until ready to use, stirring occasionally.

When the skins are ready to begin tanning, strain this bark liquid through a piece of coarse burlap into a clean barrel. Take about ten gallons more water and after pouring over the bark and stirring about to extract all the tannin possible, strain it also into the tan barrel, which should now be about three-fourths full. To this add two quarts of vinegar, stir and hang the delimed sides or strips over sticks in the usual way, with as few folds and wrinkles as possible.

Plunge and stir about to get equal effect on all parts.

As soon as the hides are put in to tan prepare a second bark liquor, using the same amount of bark and water as before.

After the hides have been in the tan ten or fifteen days, take out five gallons of the first partly spent liquor and replace it with the same amount of the second liquor and also add to it another two quarts vinegar, stirring it well. After five days add another five gallons of the second tan liquor but no vinegar, and so on every five days until it is used up.

About thirty-five days after the tanning was started, weigh out forty pounds more of ground bark and placing it in a tub just moisten it with hot water. Only use as much water as the bark will soak up.

Pull the sides out of the barrel and inspect them as to the progress of tanning. A bit cut from the edges of the hide should show a brown streak or line coming in from each surface of the hide.

While the sides are out, dump in the moistened bark, retaining as much as possible of the old liquor. Mix thoroughly and hang the sides back in the barrel, burying them in the bark mixture completely. Leave in this for six weeks with an occasional stirring. Draw the hides a second time, empty out one-half the liquor, stir well, replace the hides and fill the barrel with freshly ground bark. Leave the sides in for about two months, stirring from time to time and adding enough bark and water to keep the sides entirely covered.

At the end of this time a cut should show the hide an even color all through without any white or raw streak in the center. If it is not yet struck through it must be returned to the wet bark and more added if necessary until it is. Sole leather must be left for two months longer. Thus the time needed for tanning harness and belting leather with bark is about four and a half months, and six and a half months for sole leather. When examination shows fully tanned, the sides may be removed and well scrubbed, especially the grain side, and allowed to partly dry when they are to be finished as by other processes.

CHAPTER XIV

BUCKSKIN

TO MAKE good buckskin in Indian style required real labor but very little else. No materials or tools were used that were not at hand almost anywhere in the wilderness. Such buckskin was not, properly speaking, tanned at all, but the fibre was separated and softened by mechanical means and preserved in that condition by the application of grease and smoke. Buckskin so made dries quite stiff after wetting, but can be rendered pliable again by rubbing with the hands.

There were different modes of making buckskin practiced in various parts of the country, but in the main they followed about the same course. This consisted of, first, soaking; second, unhairing and fleshing; third, alternately soaking in a warm solution of brains, partly drying, and pulling and stretching until sufficiently pliable; fourth and finally, smoking in wood smoke, which rendered it more durable as well as improved the appearance.

111

The tools used were few and crude. A log trough answered for soaking the skins in clear water until the hair and grain would slip, then the skin was put on a peeled log and unhaired and fleshed with some such tool as a sharpened rib or other bone. The brain contents of the deer, with perhaps some other miscellaneous grease, was made into a paste in hot water and applied warm to the skin which was then allowed to partly dry when it was pulled, twisted and stretched in every direction to loosen the fibres. The hands alone were used for this, unless perhaps it might be pulled over the edge of a sharpened stump. In the partly dry state any thinning needed was done, by scraping with the edge of stones or shells in the absence of iron tools. Such thinning was chiefly done on the neck and back and, with the expenditure of a vast deal of elbow grease, brought the skin to a state of flexibility but little less than that of cloth.

The smoking was done usually on a frame of sticks over a slow fire of "punk" or dozy wood, which afforded a slow burning fire of little heat but plenty of smoke.

Well made, such buckskin is as soft as chamois leather but far stronger, warmer than cloth, and proof against briars and burrs. No tannin in any form, nor even any salt was used in the manufacture. What the Indians could do with such poor facilities white men can duplicate if they possess a large stock of patience.

The present day mode of making buckskin is practically the same, only in place of the brain paste a warm solution of soap is used. If the deer skins are soaked in clear water no neutralizing washes are needed, as in the case when lime or lye is used.

Deer hair and grain are so easy to loosen it is best to use only water, in some warm place, and watch the skins well, until ready to unhair. Then put on the beam, neck towards the workman, and push off the hair and epidermis from the entire skin. Turn flesh side up and flesh thoroughly. The neck and back may be partly shaved with a sharp knife now, and finished later when partly dry, if desired.

Take some of the home made soft soap, a pint

say, and make into a strong suds with a bucket of hot water. While it is still luke warm put the skin in and work the suds well into it; leave it in the soapy water in a warm place for four or five days. Wring out and pull and stretch it as it dries, then give it a coat of oil or grease dressing of some kind, lard, butter or bacon grease. Warm up the water and add another half pint of soap and put the skin in again for another twenty-four hours.

When you can squeeze water through the skin easily, take it out and rinse in clear water, wring out, pull and stretch as before. If not sufficiently soft repeat a third time. The skin should be fully relaxed, with no hard spots when put in the soap, and should be kept in that and worked about until the water can be *easily* squeezed through it. If you cannot readily get the soft soap, use common yellow laundry soap shaved up and dissolved in the water; a bar of it in place of a pint of soft soap.

Such a skin can be pulled, rolled, twisted and rubbed while drying until very soft.

To smoke a few buckskins, if no regular smoke house is available, a large box can be made use of, by removing top and bottom and placing it over one end of a trench connecting with a hole dug in the ground for a fireplace. The skins are to be spread on a few crosspieces, just below the top of the box, which should then be covered with boards or even canvas, except a small space at the end opposite the fireplace, to allow some draught. In this way with the fire outside it is easy to tend and it is far enough from the skins to lessen the chance of overheating them. Just keep the fire smouldering and turn the skins from time to time until they are colored a deep yellow or light brown. If the flesh sides seem rough they should be smoothed with sandpaper before smoking.

The key to making good buckskin is continuous working while drying. Lay it aside then, before it is dry and it becomes stiff and hard and must be dampened up again and reworked. It is not always necessary to soak in water to dampen skins; wrapping in damp cloths over night will relax and you will not have to wait for the excess water to dry out.

Good buckskin is not only useful for clothing, gun covers, etc., but makes very ornamental

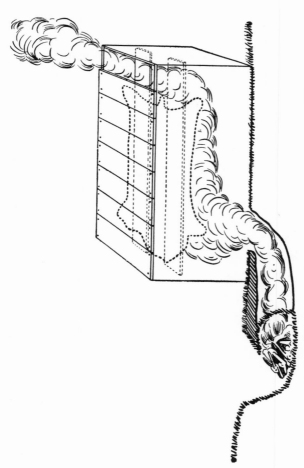

BOX, FIRE-PIT AND TRENCH, FOR SMOKING BUCKSKIN

cushion and table covers. If you wish a piece of buckskin and have no deer skin at hand try the same process on calf, sheep or goat. Sheep especially furnishes much so-called "buck" which, while it can be made into a very good leather, has not the wearing quality of the genuine.

In the early days of this country buckskin was dressed for home use as commonly as clapboards or shingles were rived from the abundant trees, but was regarded by white settlers as more or less of a make-shift, neither leather or cloth. Only Indians, hunters and shiftless people wore buckskin moccasins the year around, and buckskin was useless for harness, saddles, etc., on account of its stretching so freely when wet.

It could be made in a few days, with no special tools, a product of the temporary camp, while the real bark tanned leather was only produced after several months, belonging to a permanent residence. As a trophy of a successful hunt we think a well made buckskin is to be preferred rather than trying to dress the skin with the hair. Deer hairs become very brittle and when in use in the house break off and scatter, to the despair and disgust of the housekeeper. Then too, skins which have an imperfect coat of hair or wool will make all right buckskin.

CHAPTER XV

ROBE SKINS

ORSE and cattle hides, when selected and tanned properly, can be made into the warmest and handsomest of robes. Everyone likes to use nice furs. There is a warmth and luxury about them not to be matched by any cloth or fabric. All the ingenuity of man has never been able to produce any textile which affords such a light, warm covering as Nature's protection against the cold.

In selecting hides for robes get those with good length of hair and free from blemishes, if possible. Hides that are "spready," that is, have a large spread for their weight are preferable. The usual size robe is sixty by seventy-two inches, and one horse or cow hide of average size will make one.

It will require two or three yearlings or kips and four to eight calves, or six to ten sheep or goatskins to make such a robe. Brown or black sheep pelts with a medium or short fleece make nice robes and warm ones, too.

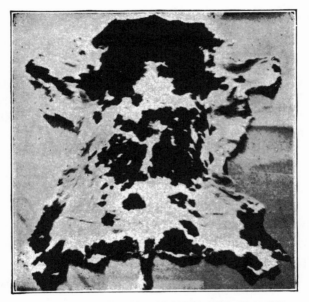

CALF SKIN, HAIR ON, FOR VEST, RUG OR ROBE

Use care in soaking robe skins not to loosen the hair or grain in any place. A good soaking solution for skins to be tanned with the hair on is made as follows:

24 gals. cold, soft water,
3 pts. soft soap,
3 oz. borax,
4½ oz. sulphuric acid.

Use one-half bar of laundry soap shaved up if you do not have the soft soap, and if the skins have not been salted put in three pints of salt. Dissolve and mix the above, adding the acid last, and place the skins in this from two to eight or ten hours. Large dry hides should soften in this over night and small or green ones need but a few hours to make them soft and flexible, ready for fleshing.

Flesh thoroughly on the beam, then wash well in clean cold water, put on the beam again and work over again to get rid of dirty water. If soft, flexible and clean, free from bits of meat and the muscular membrane on the flesh side, the skin is ready for the tanning. For this purpose use either the Oxalic Acid formula for light skins or the Sulphuric Acid formula.

For a cow or horse hide the barrel should be about one-half to three-fourths full, or say 20 to 30 gallons of liquor. As these hides are to be tanned whole, that is, without splitting into sides or strips, they cannot well be hung on the sticks but must be immersed in the liquid and frequently turned and stirred about so every part may receive equal treatment. Hides will require from a few days to a week in the tan to strike through, which can be determined by the usual test of cutting on the neck. If colored evenly quite through, remove from tan and wash in a solution of common washing soda, about one-half ounce to the gallon of water, and rinse this off in clear water.

Wring out of this and hang up until partly dry, so they will whiten when pulled, then lay on a pad on the beam or table and push in all directions with stake knife or dull flesher. When well stretched flatten by pulling and roll with the hands on table top to further soften, then while still a little damp apply a softening preparation made as follows:

Melt one pint soft soap and add one pint neatsfoot or fish oil, or even light automobile oil and one-half pint of alcohol. Apply to flesh side a coat of this warm, not hot, and rub it in well. When dry roll and work until thoroughly softened. If, when thoroughly dry there are stiff places, dampen these, oil and work dry until the skin is all soft.

If the skin was that of a cow or calf and you washed and rinsed it clean, the hair will be bright and loose when the hide is softened. If, however, you wish to dress sheep or angora goat skins with the fleece on they will require some additional treatment. After taking from the acid liquor and neutralizing, wash them out well in a strong suds of soap or washing powder, wring out of this and rinse in luke warm water.

Wring as dry as you can after rinsing and then soak in gasoline for twenty or thirty minutes, working about and squeezing the pelts so the gasoline will penetrate every part of it. Use gasoline enough to cover the skins and use it away from fires and lights; outdoors is best. In the meantime procure some corn meal, about as much in bulk as the skins to be cleaned, put it in a pan and heat it on a stove or in the oven, taking care it does not scorch and burn. After wringing the skins as free as you can from gasoline put them in a shallow box, pour the hot meal over them and with the hands work it into the fleece. Shake out and work in the meal alternately until the wool seems free of the gasoline, then hang up in the air, shaking and beating with a rattan or smooth stick until the meal is all out and the fleece dry and fluffy. Knots, tangles and burrs should be removed with a coarse comb, a horse's mane comb will answer the purpose, before the beating is finished.

After this proceed with softening the skin by stretching, greasing and breaking. Keep the grease from the wool or hair as much as possible and finally rub over flesh side with dry sawdust to remove any excess of grease or oil.

Sheep skins may also be alum tanned with the wool on using the same solution as for lace leather, but we personally prefer the acid tanning, as it tends to discourage moths and the oxalic solution will help to clean white wool. Short wool skins or those that have been shorn recently make good lining for cold weather garments or bedside rugs.

To make skins dressed with the hair or wool

on lie flat for rugs and robes it is sometimes
necessary to cut out a small gore at the back of
the front legs and just in front of the hind ones.
The skin there is usually thin and sparsely
haired, and when sewed up with an over and
over stitch on the flesh side the longer hair each
side of the seam can usually be combed over to
hide it.   After sewing up all cuts in this way,
dampen the flesh side of the tanned robe or rug
and turning it over, tack it to the floor until it
is dry again.   The tacking is done by beginning
at the neck and tacking a row of small nails
down the center of the back to the tail.   Pull the
skin back as you go along so there are no
wrinkles.   Then pull the legs out and tack them,
getting both sides to match, and finish by
stretching out the whole skin and fastening it
by a row of nails around the edge only a few
inches apart.   Begin these at the center of one
side and nail alternately one side and the other
in order to stretch them evenly.   Use wire nails
close to the margin of the skin and the holes
will not damage it; probably most of them will
be trimmed off when we remove them and trim
the dry skin to a smooth outline.

Such robes and rugs may be used without lining, though a suitable lining and border will add to their durability in some cases and to their looks in all.

BLACK BEAR SKIN, FUR ON, ROBE AND RUG MATERIAL

RAWHIDE, while not in any sense leather, is a very useful material, and the first stages of its preparation are identical.   If a fresh hide is used, soak it in either pure water or a weak lye made by a mixture of wood ashes and water until the hair slips.   A dry skin, of course, must be soaked and scraped until soft first.   When the hair scrapes off readily, unhair and flesh the hide as usual.   Then wash the hide well and stretch it to its full extent and fasten it so until dry.   This can be done by nailing on the side of a building or lacing it in a frame.   The latter way is best, as then it may be hung up inside some shed or loft out of reach of animals.   If fastened on the side of a building it had better be the inside.

In case you wish to soften a piece of rawhide it may be treated to a coat of oil and tallow, equal parts, and worked over the edge of a plank or bar.   Lacking oil and tallow almost any animal grease will do. Use no salt or salted skins for rawhide.

Rawhide can be made into buckets, baskets, telescope bags and similar things which will stand almost any amount of hard knocks and abuse in handling. To make these, cut rawhide to the pattern wanted, soak until soft and sew up with some thin strips cut from the hide. Dry them on wooden forms or fill with dry sand and let stand until dry. Handles of twisted hide should be fitted to such receptacles when they are made, to complete them. As repair material such rawhide is valuable. By binding cracked woodwork with damp rawhide it can be made nearly as strong as new, when well dried out. We have seen gun stocks repaired so and have heard of a broken wagon tire being replaced by several layers of damp rawhide, which on drying was used for several months.

Riatas or ropes may be made of rawhide, cut up as for laces and plaited. The strips are to be kept damp while working and after plaiting and stretching grease the rope thoroughly to keep it pliable.

Alligator hides, once very plentiful in the

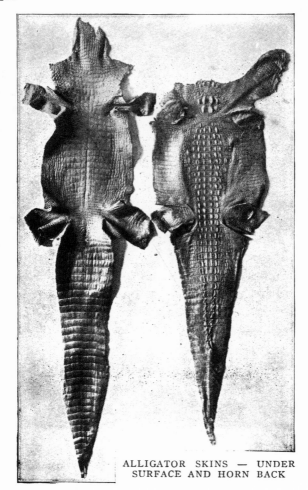

ALLIGATOR SKINS — UNDER
SURFACE AND HORN BACK

southeastern states, make a very durable as well as ornamental leather. That made of the small and medium skins being suitable for bags, suit cases, pocketbooks, etc. Of the larger specimens, only the skin along the belly and sides can be made into pliable leather; the back plates defy softening. The "gator" skins should never be allowed to dry out before tanning, but be well salted and packed in salt in tight tubs or barrels until they are tanned. Soak from two to six days according to size, until relaxed, work over flesh side and put in lime for one or two weeks. Take out of lime, scrape the thin horny scales off, flesh, drench, wash and tan as with other hides. When tanning is completed, wash and stretch until partly dry. Then dress with tallow and oil or oil alone for small skins, and 'ake until soft.

It is possible that many readers of this may ever handle a raw "gator" hide, though in recent times every swamp, river and lake in the Southland was the natural home of the alligator. He is going fast before the advance of civilization and, unlike other wild animals, there is but little sentiment to oppose an early extermination.   Alligator hunting, once a common sport

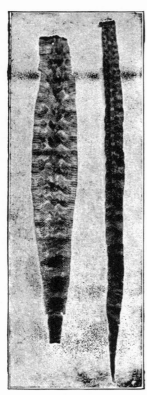

within its range, is about over; the great swamps are being drained and most of all the hide hunters have worked their will on them since fashion created a demand for such leather b a c k in 1880. The United States Fish Commission has estimated t h a t between 1880 and 1894, 2,500,000 alligators were killed in Florida alone.   One man took 800 skins in a year and another made the record of 42 in one night.

TANNED SNAKE SKINS
Rattle (left); Black (right)

Snake skins are dressed much as are alligators, and like them should be kept salted and in a damp state while awaiting tanning.   The acid processes

will tan them very nicely, but they require careful handling, as at certain times they are quite frail on account of the annual shedding or sloughing of the skin.

While leather from the smaller snakes has little durability, it is in some demand, especially from rattlesnakes, for souvenirs. By re-inforcing with other leather such light skins may be made up as belts, hat bands, pocketbooks, cigar and card cases and similar small articles. The charm of serpent leather is in its odd and beautiful scale patterns. These show up well, if after tanning the scale side of the leather is rubbed with wax and polished with a *warm*, not *hot* iron, using considerable pressure.

There are a number of by-products which regular tanners derive considerable revenue from. They handle such large numbers of hides and skins that they obtain much greater proportionate returns than one can who may tan but a few hides in a year. Still cattle hair can be used about home in mortar for plastering and for padding cushions, and wool removed from sheep pelts may be sold with the yearly clip.

The hair should be collected after scraping off and merely rinsed if to be used in plastering.

but if for upholstering it should be washed in several changes of water until absolutely clean and dried out in a warm place. If the wool from pelts has been pulled it will need considerable washing too, but if clipped it may be handled as such wool always is. The fleece from Angora goats, known as mohair, is of more value than wool and should be handled carefully.

The refuse from the liming operation, lime water, sludge and fleshings have some value as a fertilizing material, for acid soils in particular.

Hoofs and hide trimmings may be boiled down in water for many hours until the water thickens so much that when cooled it will set solid into glue. Such oil as is skimmed off in the glue making is of use in softening leather, the so-called neatsfoot or tanners' oil. Fat and tallow that adheres to hides should be saved and rendered, as the home tanner can use it.

Horns are hardly salable except in large lots to the comb factories, but can be turned into many useful and ornamental objects at home. Elegant chairs, stools and smaller novelties have been made from polished horns.

Skins of small animals killed for food and which have no value for fur, such as squirrel, woodchuck or summer coon skins make good strings and laces when prepared like rawhide and cut out before softening. Such small skins may also be tanned or treated like buckskin and used for a variety of purposes, such as facing gloves and mittens or making moccasins and slippers.

CHAPTER XVII

SALTING AND CURING HIDES

IDES and skins properly handled are worth more to the farmer, rancher, dairyman, country butcher, etc., regardless of whether they are sold to some hide buyer or turned into leather, tanned at home.

This and the following chapters are from a 56 page bulletin issued by United States Department of Agriculture, entitled Country Hides and Skins, which covers thoroughly the subjects of skinning, curing and marketing:

The next important operation after the hides and skins have been correctly removed is that of curing or preserving them in a sound condition, which is best accomplished by thorough salting.

In cold weather hides and skins may be safely kept for some time without salting, though care should be taken to prevent them from freezing. In spring, summer, and fall, however, they must be salted promptly if they are to be made into good leather and pay for the work of saving them.

SALTING AND CURING ON THE FARM

Cattle and Horse Hides. Before salting see that the hide is clean. Other factors being equal, clean hides bring the most money because there is less waste on them and they make better· leather. After the hide has been removed carefully from the animal, clean off as much as possible all remaining dirt and blood; remove any pieces of flesh by scraping with the back of a butcher knife and by careful cutting; trim off any ragged edges, and split the ears twice. Then allow the hide to lose its animal heat, in a cool, dark, dry place. Six hours is usually long enough for this, although overnight is permissible in cool weather.

For curing select a cool, clean place, preferably a cellar, or a barn floor free from drafts and out of the direct sunlight. A floor with a slight slope and a drain is the best. Sprinkle on the selected space a thin layer of clean crystal salt (about pea size) or ordinary salt of the kind used for salting meat. When the hide has cooled sufficiently spread it, hair side down, over the salted floor, being sure to straighten out all folds and laps. Sprinkle fresh, clean salt all over the flesh side of the hide, using about 1 pound of salt for every pound of hide. See that all parts of the flesh side receive a sprinkling of the salt. Be sure to use plenty of salt and rub it in well along the cut edges, head, neck, legs, wrinkles, and the heavy portions.

If several hides are to be cured, pile them one on top of another, always hair side down, with their heads at one end, and salt each one on the flesh side as directed. In piling the hides, do not drag them across the stack of salted ones, as this disturbs the salt on those underneath, causing unsalted spots and spoiled hides.

The liquor from the pile of hides must be drained away to prevent damage to the bottom ones.

In curing, the hides if properly salted will become firm and stiff, when they are known as "salt firm" or "salt hard." This requires some time, generally 6 to 14 days, after which the hides are ready for bundling and shipping. They should rarely be bundled immediately after salting.

Calfskins. After the skins have become cool, salt them in the same manner as cattle or horse hides. It is safer, however, to use a finer salt than is used for hides and to rub it in with the hands around the neck, head, tail root, legs, and shanks.

Sheepskins. Sheepskins require longer to cool. Do not salt them until thoroughly cooled, which will take from 8 to 10 hours in the summer. Use about one-half pound of clean, fine salt to 1 pound of skin, sprinkle it on by hand, and make sure that every spot on the flesh side gets some salt.

Send sheepskins and lambskins to market promptly. Hold them only 4 or 5 days, 6 at most, after salting, as they are liable to heat rapidly, causing decomposition and decrease in value if not total loss. For the same reason not more than 10 should be placed in one pile.

Dry-salted Curing. In hot, dry sections of the country, like the Southwestern States and

Mexico, hides and skins may be cured by "dry salting." Thoroughly salt the flesh side of the green or fresh hide, in accordance with the directions in the preceding paragraphs, and leave it until it has become firm and somewhat stiff, that is, "Salt firm," which requires from 6 to 12 days. Then hang up the salted hide or skin or swing it over a pole, with the flesh side out, and let it dry thoroughly under an open shed or in some place where there is a good draft of air, protected, however, from the weather. After the hide or skin has become dry, it is advisable to lightly resalt the flesh side before storing or shipping. The chief advantage in dry salting is the reduction in weight thus effected, with the consequent decrease in the cost and labor of transportation.

Keeping Cured Hides and Skins. Properly and thoroughly cured hides and skins, other than sheepskins, may be bundled and safely kept for some time in a cool place. Fall, winter, and spring hides may be kept until May. or June without undue deterioration. In this way it is often possible to collect a number sufficient for advantageous marketing. As a general rule, however, it is inadvisable to keep hides and skins over the summer.

SALTING AND CURING BY BUTCHERS

The butcher, as distinguished from the farmer, has a much larger number of hides and skins, and he can handle them advantageously in a somewhat different manner. Because of the extent of his business the butcher can afford and should have a proper place and facilities for slaughtering and for curing hides and skins.

The methods recommended to butchers for salting cattle and calfskins are as follows:

Salting is best carried out in a dry, cool room, or preferably in a cellar or even temperature and free from drafts. If many hides are to be stored the cellar should have a concrete floor and good drainage.

Before salting clean the hide thoroughly, removing the dirt, dung, and blood from both the hair and flesh sides, particularly the latter. A clean hide or skin is not so liable to spoil in spots while curing, and will sell well, as it presents a clean, bright appearance. Hides and skins are more easily freed from dung and dirt before the animals are felled, and during flaying care should be taken to keep the hides and skins from coming in contact with the blood from slaughtering. Blood spots especially damage and discolor the hide. Water should be used sparingly in cleaning the hides, and for the flesh side a clean, moistened cloth will suffice. Trim the hide nicely, removing all stringy pieces; cut off the dewclaws if any; split the ears with two cuts, and scrape away any flesh or meat, although the latter should not be present on a properly flayed hide or skin.

In allowing the animal heat to escape from the hides and skins it is permissible, if the weather is very cool, to let them lie overnight spread out singly with flesh side up. During warm weather, however, they should first be sprinkled lightly with fine salt. The questions of temperature and the right time to start salting are very important, as the hides and skins should not be salted and piled while still warm, nor should they be allowed to remain unsalted too long or decomposition will set in. This happens often but does not show up until the hides are in the tanning process.

As soon as the hide or skin has completely lost its animal heat it is ready for salting. Spread it out perfectly flat and smooth on the floor, which has been previously sprinkled with clean, coarse salt. Select, if possible, a floor having a slight incline to promote drainage. Always put the hair side down. Sprinkle the flesh side evenly with clean, coarse salt, using about a pound to a pound of hide. Be careful to salt uniformly and thoroughly and see that every spot the size of a dime has at least one grain of salt on it. Work the salt well into the heavy parts, such as the head, and also into every little place, particularly the edges. Be liberal in the use of salt; it will be economy in the end.

It is important to use clean, pure salt. Where quantities of hides and skins are handled there will soon be an accumulation of used salt which has been removed from the cured hides and skins before shipping. This old salt, if washed free from blood, dirt, and fine particles, may be used again when mixed with about twice its weight of new salt, but no old salt should be

used on packs or piles which are not to be removed for some time.   In fact, there is serious
danger of damage to hides from the use of old
salt.   New, clean, pure salt is always to be preferred.

In curing 30 to 40 or more hides or skins, they
may be placed in one stack by piling flat.   Always stack with the flesh side up and the heads
at one end.   Salt each hide or skin thoroughly
after it is placed on the pile.   In stacking, two
men are required, one at each end of the pile.
This is necessary to prevent the dragging of the
hide across the under one and so distributing the
evenly distributed salt on it.   When building
these piles, care should be taken to keep them
level.   There is a tendency for the pile to thicken
up in the middle, a tendency which limits the
number of hides that may be placed in one pile.
As soon as difficulty is experienced in keeping
the middle down a new pile should be started.

After the stack or pile has been laid, the top
hide should be liberally covered with salt, and
the sides of the pile also should be sprinkled with
it.   Hides may remain in these piles 4 to 6 weeks
before shipping.   They should not be shipped or

moved in less than 10 days. Be sure that there is proper drainage at the bottom of the pile so as not to ruin the lower hides by the liquor formed during curing.

Some butchers make a practice, before stacking, of "banking" the hides and skins for from 24 to 48 hours, and from their experience better cured hides, free from salt stains, are obtained. The object of banking is to give the salted hides and skins an opportunity to drain off the excess moisture and blood. A simple type of bank is an inclined platform with the rear end raised about 18 inches from the floor. The platform should be practically 12 feet long and of a width depending on the number of hides and skins handled at one time; each pile of hides will require about 8 feet.

The hides or skins are spread out smoothly on the platform, always flesh side up and with the heads at the lower end of the incline. Each one is well sprinkled with salt on the flesh side after it has been laid out on the platform. From 25 to 50 hides can be piled safely, one on top of the other. The hides and skins are allowed to lie on the bank from one to two days, after which they are piled or packed as previously described. When transferring the hides and skins from the bank to the pile, it will be necessary to sprinkle a little more salt over each one as it is laid on the pile. A careful watch should be kept for unsalted spots or sections not well supplied with salt, and if any are found they should be completely covered with salt.

While the salting of calfskins and yearlings is practically the same as for cattle hides, some recommend the use of medium-fine salt for the first two. This is a good plan to follow, although the use of finer salt is not necessary. Horsehides may be salted in exactly the same way as cattle hides.

Sheepskins, however, require the use of fine salt. They must also be allowed a little more time to cool off, and should not be kept more than five or six days after salting, since they have a tendency to heat very quickly and easily. For the same reason it is advisable not to put more than 10 in one pile.

Protecting Stored Hides Against worms and Bugs. Cured hides and skins are often attacked by insects and worms during storage and transportation. This is especially true in the case of dried hides and skins not cured with salt and of those in tropical or semi-tropical countries. Various preparations, the so-called "hide poisons," are applied as a protection against insects and worms. Many of these preparations are covered by patents which contain complete instructions as to the methods of application.

As a rule, the poison is applied by sprinkling the solution over the hair where the insects are found. A light application on the flesh side will do no harm. Arsenious acid in alkaline solution, potassium cyanide, carbolic-acid creosote, naphthols, naphthalenese, and the like are used for this purpose. As most of the "hide poisons" are deadly poisons, the utmost care must be exercised in handling them.

Modern American Tanning gives the following directions for making "hide poison:"

Dissolve 40 pounds of red or white arsenic and 1 pound of concentrated lye with water in a kerosene barrel. Allow this mixture to stand for one week. Two pailfuls of this mixture, poured into an oil barrel full of water, give a solution ready for use.

It has been recommended that dried hides and skins to be stored in piles or shipped in bundles be sprinkled with naphthalene to keep them free from insects and to prevent heating.   Some members of the trade consider it inadvisable to spray dry sheepskins with arsenic solution, as it stains the wool.   They maintain that properly dried sheepskins can be kept satisfactorily if they are carefully and thoroughly sprinkled with naphthalene.

CHAPTER XVIII

PREPARING HIDES AND SKINS FOR MARKET

HEN about to ship cured hides and skins of the green-salted description, place them over some elevated object, such as a barrel; allow them to remain there overnight to drain free of excess moisture; after which free them of surplus salt by sweeping or thorough shaking. The latter is usually done five times on each side, over a solidly constructed, slightly elevated rack made of heavy timbers which are set far enough apart to permit the salt to escape readily to the floor. If hides are handled as directed, the shrinkage should be relatively small when they are weighed at the hide house.

FOLDING AND BUNDLING HIDES AND SKINS

The steps generally followed in folding and bundling hides for shpiment will be easily understood by studying the accompanying diagrams, figures 41 and 42, in which the hair side is designated by shading. As a rule hides are folded so that the hair side is out.

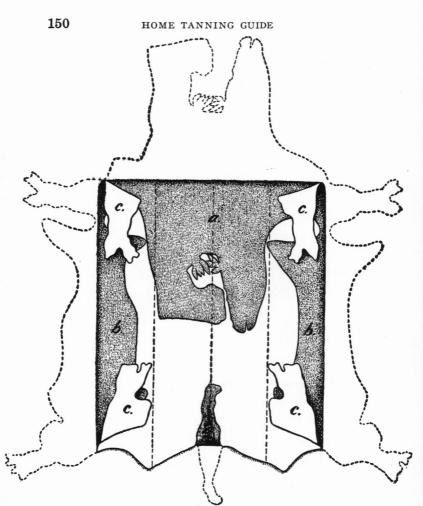

Fig. 41—FOLDING AND BUNDLING HIDES—BEGINNING
A, First Step; B, Second Step; C, Third Step.

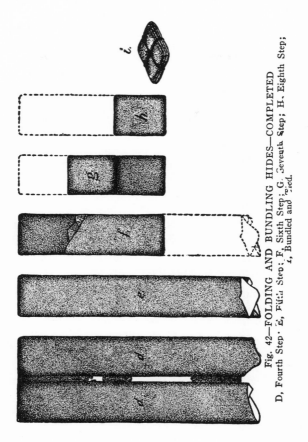

Fig. 42—FOLDING AND BUNDLING HIDES—COMPLETED
D, Fourth Step; E, Fifth Step; F, Sixth Step; G, Seventh Step; H, Eighth Step; I, Bundled and Tied.

HOW TO FOLD A HIDE

1—Fold in the head and neck on the body of the hide, flesh surfaces together, and turn in the tail, as shown by fold *a*.

2—Make a narrow fold on each side by throwing the belly edges and legs upon the body of the hide, flesh surfaces together, keeping the lines of the fold parallel, as shown by *b*.

3—Fold the legs back on these laps, hair surfaces together. See folds *c*.

4—Bring the break of each fold near the middle line of the back, as shown by folds *d*.

5—Complete the side folds by bringing the two breaks of the folds thus made together, with the middle line of the back as the main fold, thus making one long, rectangular bundle, as shown in *e*.

6—Throw the butt end of the folded hide forward about four-fifths of the distance to the neck fold. See *f*.

7—Fold the forward portion of the bottom lap back on top of the first fold. See *g*.

8—Bring the break of the rear fold even with that of the fold just made. This makes a neat, square bundle, ready for tying. See *h*.

Each hide is bundled separately and tied securely. About 7 feet of strong cord will be needed to tie one hide bundle. A soft rope or line at least a quarter of an inch thick will answer the purpose well, though regular hide rope is preferred. Information regarding suitable rope, the nearest source of supply, and approximate prices may be obtained from hide dealers. Tie the bundle tightly by passing the rope around it in two directions. See *i* in figure 42. Wire should never be used, as it is liable to damage the hide by rusting.

Calfskins are folded in exactly the same way as cattle hides. However, when more than one are to be shipped place two folded skins together and tie into one bundle instead of tying each one separately.

Sheepskins are bundled differently from either cattle hides or calfskins. Lay the wool sides down, and fold the skins along the median line of the back, having the wool side out. As many as five skins folded in this manner can be placed in a single bundle for shipment. It is not advisable to place more than that number in one bundle, as the wool helps to generate heat very rapidly. Two pieces of stout rope are then wound around the pack from back to belly, one passing around the back portion just in front of the hind legs and the other passing around the front portion immediately back of the forelegs.

All bundles must be tied securely, and in making knots the nautical bowline knot is preferable, as it does not slip easily. Bundles often become untied or otherwise lose their identification marks, and in such cases the railroad employees have no means of determining the identity of either shipper or consignee, especially if there are other hide shipments in the car.

TAGGING

Each bundle should be tagged securely with the name and address of the dealer to whom shipped on one side of the tag, and on the other side, after the word 'From —," the name and address of the shipper. Be sure the tag can not come off. Ordinary paper tags are not safe, as they are too easily destroyed or pulled off. Good, strong linen tags with a paper finish and brass eyelets are preferred. All addressing should be done plainly in ink. Pencil marks often become illegible. Remember that if the bundle becomes unwrapped or if the tag pulls off, the hides and skins are liable to be lost.

SHIPPING

After the hides and skins have been properly and securely bundled and tagged ship them without delay.   Do not let the bundle remain in the sun, draft, or water, or against rusty or corroding metals.   Promptness in shipping is always advisable, but applies particularly to sheepskins.   They heat rapidly after being bundled, and in hot weather especially must reach their destination quickly.

Hides and skins should be shipped directly, if practicable, to reliable hide dealers who sell direct to tanners, thus eliminating unnecessary middlemen or agents.   Repeated handlings tend to reduce the quality.   For most farmers, ranchmen, and small butchers it would, no doubt, be desirable if they could dispose of their hides and skins immediately after removal, without salting and curing them.   As a rule, however, this is entirely impracticable, since only a few are near enough to tanneries or dealers equipped to handle their products.   When so favorably sit-

uated producers doubtless will find it both profitable and practicable to sell the hides and skins in
the green, unsalted condition.   In no case, however, should this method be considered unless
the producer is absolutely certain of delivering
the green hides and skins promptly, within, as a
safe rule, 24 hours after skinning.   Otherwise
any benefits that might be derived will be more
than offset by deterioration and decay.

At all times, and especially in warm weather,
it is impracticable to ship green hides and skins
any distance.   They will taint and putrefy almost as easily as fresh meat.   If they must be
shipped at once they should be salted heavily
enough to prevent deterioration in transit.   Be-
sides the great chance for loss from decomposition, the requirements of the express companies
that all green hides and skins be shipped in
tight boxes, barrels, or kegs, make this method
unprofitable, because of the expense of these
containers and of the extra cost of transportation.

CHAPTER XIX

MARKET CLASSES OF HIDES AND SKINS

OST farmers and ranchmen and many local butchers are unfamiliar with the specifications for the various market classes and grades of hides and skins with their relative values and the corresponding market price. Such knowledge would place the country-hide producer on a more equal footing with the buyer and enable him to demand and receive prices in accordance with the quality of his products. Misunderstanding and suspicion, which serve only to handicap the industry, also would be less frequent.

CLASSES, GRADES, AND SELECTIONS OF PACKER HIDES AND SKINS

With a few minor changes in the descriptions, the data given below are the same as those issued in 1918 by the War Industries Board.

GRADES

Grubs. During certain times of the year, hides and skins often are damaged by grub holes and bceause of this a selection or grading based on the number of grub holes is generally made during the grubbing season. Packer hides with fewer than 5 grub holes are graded as No. 1, while those with 5 or more are graded as No. 2. The grubbing seasons are as follows: On Texas steers and branded cows, from November 1 to June 1; on Colorados, from December 1 to June 1; on native steers (including "spreadies"), "butt-brands," and native cows, from January 1 to June 1.

Hair Slips and Cuts. Packer hides are graded as No. 1 except when there are hair slips or a cut in the body of the hide which can not be trimmed out without spoiling the pattern. Such hides are classed as No. 2 or as glue stock, depending upon the extent of the damage. A No. 2 hide generally sells at 1 cent a pound less than a No. 1 hide of similar class and weight.

There is no exact definition for glue hides. Generally hides that are tainted, have hair slips or many grub holes, or are of extremely irregular pattern are in this class.

CLASSES

Native steers are unbranded steer hides, native meaning simply unbranded. They are selected as follows and are sold as such regardless of place of origin.

Spready native steers are steer hides free from brands, weighing 60 pounds and up and measuring 6½ feet and over just behind the brisket. From June to December, inclusive, they are sold as No. 1 only. During January to May, inclusive, they are sold on a grub selection. The koshers of this selection may be sold on the same measurements, or 6 feet 8 inches and over, according to custom.

Heavy native steers are heavy, unbranded steer hides, weighing 60 pounds and up. They are graded No. 1 and No. 2.

Light native steers are unbranded steer hides weighing from 50 to 60 pounds. They are graded as No. 1 and No. 2.

Extreme light native steers are unbranded steer hides weighing from 25 to 50 pounds. They are graded as No. 1 and No. 2.

Texas steers are small, close-pattern, plump, branded steer hides. Originally they were from cattle coming from the ranges of Texas and vicinity, but now are sold as such regardless of place of origin. At Fort Worth, however, all branded steer hides are classed as Texas steers.

Heavy Texas steers are specially selected, branded steer hides weighing 60 pounds and up. They are graded as No. 1 and No. 2.

Light Texas steers are specially selected, branded steer hides weighing from 50 to 60 pounds. They are graded as No. 1 and No. 2.

Extreme light Texas steers are specially selected, branded steer hides weighing from 25 to 50 pounds. They are graded as No. 1 and No. 2.

Butt-branded steers are steer hides which carry one or more brands on the rump and are sold as one class without regard to origin.

Heavy butt-branded steers are butt-branded steer hides weighing 60 pounds or over. They are graded as No. 1 and No. 2.

Light butt-branded steers are butt-branded steer hides weighing from 50 to 60 pounds. They are graded as No. 1 and No. 2.

Extreme light butt-branded steers are butt-branded steer hides weighing from 25 to 50 pounds. They are graded as No. 1 and No. 2. Selection is seldom made for this grade, as they are usually sold in with extreme light Texas steer hides or with light butt-branded hides.

Colorado steers are western side-branded steer hides generally from range cattle and usually are more spready and less plump than the Texas steer. They are so classed irrespective of their origin.

Heavy Colorado steers are western side-branded steer hides weighing 60 pounds and up. They are graded as No. 1 and No. 2.

Light Colorado steers weigh from 30 to 60 pounds. They are quoted as No. 1 and No. 2.

Native cows are unbranded cowhides.

Heavy native cowhides weigh 55 pounds and up. They are graded as No. 1 and No. 2.

Light native cowhides weigh from 25 to 55 pounds. They are graded as No. 1 and No. 2.

Branded cows are both butt and side-branded

cowhides. They are not selected on a weight basis, and are graded as No. 1 and No. 2.

Native bulls are bull hides free of brands. They are not selected on a weight basis and are graded as No. 1 and No. 2.

Branded bulls are branded bull hides and are sold flat for all weights 25 pounds and over. They are graded as No. 1 and No. 2.

Kipskins are heavy calfskins weighing from 15 to 25 pounds. They are graded as No. 1 and No. 2.

Branded kipskins are skins carrying side or butt brands. They are graded as No. 1 and No. 2.

Heavy calfskins weigh from 8 to 15 pounds. They are graded as No. 1 and No. 2.

Light calfskins weigh from 7 to 8 pounds. They are graded as No. 1 and No. 2.

Deacon skins are from newly born calves.

Slunk skins are from stillborn calves.

"Koshers" or *"cutthroats"* are hides and

skins from "koshered" cattle or cattle killed according to the requirements of the Jewish religion. They are classed and graded as other hides and skins, but usually sell for one-half a cent a pound less, because of the marred pattern due to cutting the throat crosswise instead of lengthwise.

CLASSES, GRADES, AND SELECTIONS OF COUNTRY HIDES AND SKINS

The grade terms employed in marketing country hides and skins are somewhat indefinite and are not uniformly understood and applied throughout the United States. At present there is no recognized standard of classification uniform for hides and skins originating in all sections of the country. This is due partly to former haphazard methods of marketing and partly to the alleged differences in the quality and condition of these products in different sections of the country. It is said that the conditions which produce these differences are noticeable especially in the grain texture, thickness, spread, and quality of the leather, and that they are caused largely by climatic conditions, methods of hand

ling cattle, kinds of cattle, kinds of feed, methods of feeding, ticks, grubs, brands, environ-
ment, and the methods employed in skinning,
curing, and marketing the hides. Because of
these conditions the hide trade has divided the
United States into sections, and generally dis-
criminates in the prices accordingly.

This situation has been a severe handicap for
country hides and skins in competition with the
packers' products, which may have come directly
from the same section as the country hide. In
classifying country hides and skins and estab-
lishing maximum prices for them, the War Industries Board recognized these sectional
groups and fixed a maximum price for each ten-
tative grade in each section. The sections appear below about in the order of their relative
importance as indicated by the official price list
of the War Industries Board.

NINE SECTIONS OF THE UNITED STATES RECOG-
NIZED IN THE HIDE TRADE

1. Ohio, Indiana, Pennsylvania, West Virginia, and Michigan.
2. Kentucky, Tennessee, Maryland, North
   Carolina, Virginia, and District of Colum-
   bia.

3. Maine, Vermont, New Hampshire, Massachusetts, New York, Connecticut, Rhode Island, Delaware, and New Jersey.

4. Illinois, Kansas, Missouri, Iowa, Nebraska, Wisconsin, Minnesota, and eastern parts of North Dakota and South Dakota.

5. California, Utah, Oregon, Washington, Nevada, and Idaho.

6. Texas, Oklahoma, Arkansas, and Louisiana west of the Mississippi River.

7. Florida, Alabama, Mississippi, Georgia, South Carolina, and Louisiana east of the Mississippi River.

8. Colorado, Wyoming, Montana, and western parts of North Dakota and South Dakota.

9. Arizona and New Mexico.

The following classifications and definitions apply to country hides and skins:

Heavy native steers are unbranded steer hides weighing 60 pounds or over. They are graded as No. 1 and No. 2.

Light native steers are unbranded steer hides weighing 50 to 60 pounds. They are graded as No. 1 and No. 2.

Heavy native cows are heavy, unbranded cowhides weighing 60 pounds and up. They are graded as No. 1 and No. 2.

Buffs are unbranded steer, cow, and bull hides weighing from 45 to 60 pounds. They are graded as No. 1 and No. 2. (In some sections butt-branded hides of these weights are included in the No. 2 grade.)

Extremes (*extreme lights*) are unbranded hides weighing from 25 to 45 pounds. They are graded as No. 1 and No. 2. (Butt-branded hides of these weights are included in the No. 2 grade in some sections.)

Heavy bulls (also heavy native bulls) are heavy, unbranded bull hides weighing 60 pounds and up. They are graded as No. 1 and No. 2.

Heavy branded bulls are side or butt-branded bull hides weighing 60 pounds and up. They are graded as No. 1 and No. 2.

Branded hides are side or butt-branded hides, or both. Usually they are range and Texas hides. They are sold flat for all weights from

25 pounds up, and are graded as No. 1 and No. 2.

Kipskins are heavy calfskins weighing from 15 to 25 pounds, except in the southeastern and western coast sections, where the weight range is from 15 to 30 pounds. They are graded as No. 1 and No. 2.

Heavy calf are calfskins weighing from 8 to 15 pounds. They are graded as No. 1 and No. 2.

Light calf are calfskins weighing from 7 to 8 pounds and are graded as No. 1 and No. 2.

Deacons are skins from very young calves. As a rule they weigh less than 7 pounds.

The War Industries Board in 1918 issued the following data in connection with its regulation of trading in hides and skins:

The following applies to the selection of all country hides which are sold on the basis that they are free of ticks and brands. (Ticky and branded hides are not classed as No. 2 in sections where the maximum prices already allow for same.) The price of No. 2 hides is 1 cent per pound under the No. 1 price.

No. 2 hide description:

Any cut over 6 inches in from the edge.

Over 5 bad scores (cuts not extending through the hide).

Butt brands.

5 grubs.

1 grain slip.

1 rubbed area where the grain is gone.

1 dragged area where the grain is gone.

1 sore area where the grain is gone.

A No. 1 hide must be not only of good pattern and trim (page 23), but must also be free from any one of the above-mentioned faults.

CHAPTER XX

METHODS OF MARKETING HIDES AND SKINS

WHILE improvement of country hides and skins and consequent increase in returns for them are possible, yet even with hides and skins similar in quality to those produced by the packers it is not possible for the individual producer, who must operate on a small scale and market more or less indirectly, to receive the top prices paid to the packers, who generally sell directly to the tanners.

The tannery is generally the destination of all hides and skins, and efficient and economic marketing will place them at the tannery door at the earliest practicable date in the best condition possible and with the aid of only the essential marketing agencies. Each tannery, however, as a rule, specializes in certain kinds of leather, and consequently must have uniformity in its supply of hides and skins. Since the tanner is not in position to handle all kinds and classes of these materials, some central collecting and classifying agency is necessary.

It is here that the packers have an incalculable marketing advantage over the country-hide producers. The packers deal in large numbers of hides and skins, and as a result can assort and classify them in marketable lots and sell them directly to the tanner or with the occasional intervention of only one agency, namely, the hide broker or tanner's buyer. The extremely scattered sources and the comparatively small individual production of country hides and skins make it impossible for the country-hide producers to obtain this advantage. These widely scattered materials first must be collected and classified in large lots. Consequently, before reaching the consumer or tanner they pass through many hands, each one of which exacts its toll.

The marketing of country hides and skins is characterized by a large amount of lost motion. Many of the present systems support expensive, nonessential, wasteful, profit-absorbing and speculating intermediaries, which operate, possibly unintentionally but inevitably, to suppress this branch of the industry and to discourage the quality of workmanship upon which values so largely depend. The most direct and practical manner of marketing by the producer should result in the greatest profits to him.

MARKET PRICES

Three distinct fields of inquiry feature prominently in a study of present price conditions affecting the hide and leather industries. First, the difference between the prices of raw and finished products; second, the difference of 4 to 10 cents a pound between the market prices for comparable classes and grades of country and packer hides and skins; and, third, the difference of 5 to 15 cents a pound between the prices received for these products by some farmers and small butchers and those quoted for them on the market.

The unusual price conditions affecting the raw and finished products involve factors that are peculiar to periods of general economic disturbances and are not confined to the products of the hide and leather industries.

When consulting market quotations or estimating the probable values of fresh hides or skins, farmers and small butchers should bear in mind that the quality and consequent prices

of these products vary with the seasons in
which they are removed from the animal, and
that the market quotations are average prices
for large lots of cured and carefully selected
hides and skins which have shrunk from 12 to
20 per cent from the green weight, and not for
a single hide or for small lots of hides. They
also should remember that the prices that they
may receive will depend largely upon the kinds
and number of dealers or agencies that handle
their products through the various marketing
channels and on the speculative features that
may obtain when these products finally reach
the central markets.

CARELESS HANDLING AND QUESTIONABLE PRACTICES PENALIZED IN MARKETS

Another serious factor in the country-hide
situation is an evil reputation, frequently de-
served at present, but which persists even in
meritorious cases. Many farmers, ranchmen,
and small butchers, who see only the value of the
meat on the animals which they slaughter, treat
the hides and skins indifferently and carelessly,
and look upon them as waste products for which

any price is so much clear gain. Then, too, some of the traders and producers often resort to un· necessary and questionable uses of salt, pickle, and other chemicals in order to prevent shrinkage, to add false weight, or to replace the weight lost through natural shrinkage. Applying water to green-salted hides just priod to their sale for the purpose of adding weight is an equally reprehensible practice.

These questionable and dishonest practices do not deceive experienced hide buyers and tanners, who demand liberal reductions in tare and in prices when purchasing hides thus treated. There does result, however, a national economic loss, since by this ill treatment the greatest usefulness of these hides and skins is destroyed. Such treatment serves only to invite penalties in the form of low prices, not only for those sold at the time but also for future offerings, as dealers, brokers, and tanners, remembering the defective hides and skins and anticipating more, make their price arrangements as a matter of protection. Often these prices are inequitable. because the penalties generally are spread over all hides of the country description.

Because of the existence very generally of these inferior qualities, of the lack of careful selection and classification, and of the apparent inclination of many persons connected with the trade to magnify and to capitalize alleged defects, many of the country-hide producers feel that no amount of precaution and efficiency on their part would be rewarded by better prices. Though some of them realize that hides have values and that these values depend largely on carefulness and efficiency in skinning and curing, they often, because of the evil repute of country hides and skins as a class, fail to find a ready market at reasonable prices, even tho the hides they offer have been handled properly.

SELECTED AND GRADED SALES COMPARED WITH FLAT SALES

When a producer is paid as much for hides and skins which have cuts, scores, fleshings, horns, dewclaws, tail bones, sinews, hair slips, salt stains, poor pattern and trim, dragged spots, brands, grubs, and other imperfections as for those which are comparatively perfect, he is paid a premium for inefficiency and has no incentive to improve his methods or to strive for greater conservation. This applies to a less extent when hides are sold on a graded basis with only light penalties for the results of carelessness.

No farmer would sell a fat steer for the price of an old cow. There is no more reason for selling perfect hides and imperfect ones at the same price, for the chances are that the price will be on the basis of the inferior ones.

The hitherto almost universal practice of selling country hides and skins at prices without regard to selections and grades based upon quality, weight, and condition has contributed in a large way to the present condition of country hides and skins, with the consequent tanner's aversion to them and the wide margin between the market prices of such hides and of packer hides. The practice of flat selling is not suited to modern methods of marketing and has been abandoned by all progressive producers and merchants in nearly every line of merchandise.

A long stride forward was made when the War Industries Board in 1918 issued orders requiring all hides and skins to be sold by classes and grades. The maximum results of this progressive measure, however, will be deferred until the various methods of grading have been revised, simplified, correlated, and faithfully applied to the trading in all sections of the country. There should be well-defined classes and grades, not only for packer but also for country hides and skins. In fact, a single standard for all hides and skins by means of which they can be graded and sold on merit, regardless of origin, is desirable, and deserves serious consideration. A standardized basis for trading should make it possible for the country producers to realize prices more commensurate with the quality of their products. As a result, carelessness and much inefficiency should soon be overcome and a marked improvement in the merchantability and market prices of hides and skins of the country class should follow.

Home Manufacture of Furs and Skins

A book of practical instructions telling how to tan, dress, color and manufacture or make into articles of ornament; use or wear.

THE author, who has been in close touch with trappers, hunters and other outdoor people for more than twenty years as a practical tanner, furrier and taxidermist in the introduction says: "Probably one of the oldest human industries is Home Dressing and Manufacturing of Furs and Skins, as this method of clothing the body has persisted from the early days (even back to the stone age) to the present time. As a happy combination of dress and ornament will always continue to lead. At the present time the manufacture of furs has been highly developed, with the aid of machinery and specialized workmen it is conducted on a scale which compares favorably with any business activity. However, the principles remain the same, and good results can still be attained by hand labor. To the average outdoor man it is a positive pleasure to see the stiff, dirty, raw skin develop into the soft, clean, flexible material, and later to shape it into a protection from the cold and an ornament combined."

This new, practical and only book on the subject contains 285 pages, 91 illustrations, 34 chapters, and offers at a small cost a way for you to learn a pleasant and profitable business enabling you to tan, dye, dress and manufacture not only your own catch but to engage in the business if you wish. Read the chapter headings, which will show you how complete the book is:

If you like to handle furs, skins and hides HOME MANUFACTURE OF FURS AND SKINS will show you how to make more money out of your catch or buy by tanning, dyeing and manufacturing into articles for which there is usually a ready market at prices much higher than the raw skins will bring. This book like others on hunting, trapping, etc., that I publish is practical and written so that it is easily understood.

A.R. HARDING PUB. CO.   2878 E. Main St., Columbus, Ohio 43209